The Autobiography of Thomas Jefferson,

1743–1790

The Autobiography of Thomas Jefferson,

1743–1790

Together with a Summary of the
Chief Events in Jefferson's Life

Edited by
PAUL LEICESTER FORD

New Introduction by
MICHAEL ZUCKERMAN

PENN

University of Pennsylvania Press
Philadelphia

Originally published 1914 by G. P. Putnam's Sons
Introduction copyright © 2005 University of Pennsylvania Press
Printed in the United States of America on acid-free paper

10 9 8 7 6 5 4 3 2 1

Published 2005 by
University of Pennsylvania Press
Philadelphia, Pennsylvania 19104-4011

Library of Congress Cataloging-in-Publication Data

Jefferson, Thomas, 1743–1826.
  The autobiography of Thomas Jefferson, 1743–1790 : together with a
summary of the chief events in Jefferson's life / edited by Paul Leices-
ter Ford ; new introduction by Michael Zuckerman.
    p. cm.
  Originally published: New York : G.P. Putman's Sons, 1914. With new
introd.
  ISBN 0-8122-1901-5 (pbk. : alk. paper)
  1. Jefferson, Thomas, 1743–1826. 2. Presidents—United States—
Biography. I. Ford, Paul Leicester, 1865–1902. II. Title.
E332.9.A8 2004
973.4'6'092—dc22   2004043125
[B]

CONTENTS

INTRODUCTION

—

MICHAEL ZUCKERMAN

Benjamin Franklin and Thomas Jefferson. In their time, our two great players on the world stage, very nearly our only players of any international reputation or consequence. Ever since, our avatars of the American dream. The Philadelphian fully thirty-seven years older than the Virginian, yet the two of them twinned in our national imagination as they were twined in the crafting the Declaration of Independence and the American Philosophical Society, and in finding the passionate love of their lives in Paris.

Benjamin Franklin and Thomas Jefferson. Cultivating correspondences and keeping company with the finest minds of the Old World: artists and aristocrats, scientists and philosophers, rulers and revolutionaries. Attracting the statesmen and seers of the great courts of Europe, who found their conversation fascinating, and not just in the patronizing way that worldly sophisticates indulge earnest provincials. Proving themselves—discovering themselves—as informed, ingenious, and inventive as anyone they encountered in the coffeehouses of London or the salons of Paris.

Franklin an impossible act to follow. The most celebrated scientist of the eighteenth century. The greatest diplomat, on the most urgent of diplomatic mis-
sions, in all of American history. Literally, the most
famous man in the world. His image everywhere: in
paintings, prints, statuettes, and busts, on cup and
saucer sets, snuffboxes, ashtrays, andirons, wallpaper,
elaborate models we might now call action figures,
even an equivocally handsome Chevres chamber-pot.
His face, he said, almost as well known as that of the
moon.

Jefferson appointed to the embassy to France in
Franklin's stead. Able to succeed Dr. Franklin, he
liked to say, but not to replace him. Mistaken. Exactly like Franklin, America's minister to France and the
New World's ambassador to the Old. Both of them
embodiments of Europe's fondest fantasies of a universal enlightenment, reaching even the savage shores
of other continents. Each of them savant and scientist,
connoisseur of culture and fine wines, a man with a
way with words.

In Paris and at Versailles, Jefferson too became a
confidant of great men of state. He attended daily on
the fateful debates of the States General in the year of
the French Revolution. He was "much acquainted
with the leading patriots of the assembly." As he put
it, he "had [their] confidence." After the fall of the
Bastille, the chairman of the National Assembly's
committee to form a constitution invited him to join in
the committee's deliberations. At a critical juncture in
those deliberations, the Marquis de Lafayette asked

him to host a private meeting of the leaders of the assembly. It was at Jefferson's house, in a meeting that lasted far into the evening, that those men hammered out the principles that shaped the constitution of the first French republic.

No one replaced Jefferson, then or ever after. He and Franklin remain, to this day, our incomparable inspirations, our incarnations of our best ideals. They are what we would wish to be in what Jefferson called our pursuit of happiness.

On just that account, we recur to them over and over again. Franklin's (too-) witty compaction of Poor Richardisms, *The Way to Wealth*, is even now the most widely reprinted work in the annals of American authorship. Jefferson's Declaration of Independence is still our secular scripture, and his writings on church and state and freedom of speech and press are still central if not canonical for politicians, pundits, and Supreme Court justices. We take for granted that we might still learn from them.

If we would learn, it would seem that we could not hope for better texts than their own autobiographies. There, surely, they would gather for us the harvest of their insatiable curiosity. There, surely, they would distill for us the lessons of their long, eventful lives.

Franklin's autobiography fulfills its promise and exceeds it. Though put together in patches over two decades, its coherences irradiate its odd disjointedness. Acclaimed from its first appearance, it remains to this day our classic American confession, and easily our most influential and widely read.

Still, it disappoints. It is, or at least it appears to be, preoccupied with the paltry. It is resolute in its confinement to the quotidian. It seems on its surface little more than a succession of trifling incidents. Franklin's petty disputes with his brother. His floundering faux pas on his first arrival in Philadelphia. His intrigues with friends and fellow workers. His little club of ambitious young men. On and on. Episode after episode, on matters about which we would know nothing and care nothing if he had not included them in his reminiscences.

The memoir keeps its counsel on the great deeds that defined the nation. It is silent on the Stamp Act and the Continental Congress. It does not speak of declaring independence, winning the French alliance, or negotiating the treaty that established a new nation. It reveals nothing of the work of the constitutional convention of 1787.

Franklin could have told us of his part in those stirring scenes if he had wanted to do so. Though he wrote the first portion of his memoir in 1771, when he still considered himself very much a Briton, he wrote the last three parts in the 1780s, after the Declaration that he had helped to draft and the peace that he had helped to secure. Indeed, he wrote the last two parts in 1788 and 1789, after the ratification of the Constitution that he had also helped to draft and secure.

Historians have often regretted his reticence. His account of his life, ending as it does so many decades before his death, seems strangely aborted. It does not even describe his conduct in, let alone provide his perspective on, the struggle for independence. It leaves us to long for his insight into the emergence of the young republic.

Thomas Jefferson takes up, in this autobiography, all that Franklin does not. He recalls the imperial crisis, the writing of the Declaration, his wartime governorship of Virginia, and his diplomatic service in France. His is the memoir that should have become our canonical personal account of the era of the American founding. His is the one retrospect that has it all: a great man and a great writer, writing of momentous actions and ideas.

None of the other Founding Fathers of enduring stature wrote anything to compare. Tom Paine was, like Franklin, a great writer who did not write autobiographically about the new nation he helped to shape. Alexander Hamilton never recorded his recollections of the Revolution, and neither did George Washington, who was not a great writer in any case.

Yet Jefferson's memoir has not come down to us as the essential Founder's version of the making of the nation. It does not even stand among our beloved autobiographies. In fact, it has hardly had an audience at all. Its very existence has been virtually unknown, even to scholars of American history. It languished in manuscript for a decade before it was included in a four-volume edition of Jefferson's writings and correspondence and then, a generation later, in a nine-volume edition of his works. It was not printed as a stand-alone publication until the end of the nineteenth century. Sales of that first pro-

duction were so discouraging that there was not
another one for sixty years. That second, paperback
version sold strongly for a while, but within less than
two decades the autobiography disappeared again.
Except in encompassing collections of Jefferson's
works, it has been out of print for more than three
decades.

By contrast, Franklin's autobiography is currently
available in nineteen freestanding texts: seven mass
market paperbacks, eight hardcover editions (one in
the Modern Library series), a large-type volume, a
CD-ROM, a restoration of a fair copy, and a paperback
with accompanying audio compact disk.

The disparities in the careers of the two memoirs
are as befuddling as the similarities in their composition are uncanny. Both autobiographies were written
when their authors were very old men. In a time when
males who survived childhood could not expect to live
much past fifty, Franklin lived into his eighty-fifth
year, Jefferson into his eighty-fourth. Franklin wrote
the most famous part of his autobiography when he
was seventy-eight, Jefferson the entirety of his when
he was seventy-seven. Franklin confined his account
to the first forty-eight years of his life, Jefferson to the
first forty-seven of his.

It is hard not to be puzzled. Jefferson's autobiography was so like Franklin's in so many ways, and it had
the ingredients of an imperishable success besides.
Why was it, and why has it remained, so obscure? Why
have we not treasured it as our indispensable testimo-
ny of the Revolutionary era? Why has it faded from

sight, while Franklin's memoir has served us steadily as our instruction manual on the use of the republic?

Answers to such questions are not obvious. Jefferson's narrative may be, for him, a pedestrian performance, but even if it offered nothing more than the Virginian's version of the birth of the nation, it should have had—and should still have—our grateful attention. In fact, it offers us much more.

It is studded with incident and episode, some of obvious consequence, others—such as his devising of our dollar-and-decimal monetary system—of incidental but irresistible interest. It is strewn with sprightly, penetrating observations of character, some of surpassing generosity, others—such as his portrait of Marie Antoinette and his asides on Patrick Henry and King George III—of startling frankness.

It is punctuated with perceptions and wry aperçus that could have been written yesterday. ("If the present Congress errs in too much talking, how can it be otherwise in a body to which the people send 150 lawyers, whose trade it is to question everything, yield nothing, and talk by the hour?") And it is dotted with vignettes that still speak to us though they presume upon a world we have lost.

Take Jefferson's account of his campaign to disestablish the Anglican Church in Virginia. To the time of the Revolution, most Americans knew nothing of what we now take for granted as freedom of religion. They lived in colonies, and then in states, which ordained by law the support of one Protestant denomination over all others (and forbade by law the practice of Catholicism). The autobiography describes the bitter battles to "abolish [this] spiritual tyranny." It recounts a struggle that lasted a decade and left us a legacy that has lasted centuries. But it does more than merely rehearse what Jefferson called "the severest contests in which I have ever been engaged." It reveals the fragility of popular support for the principle of separation of church and state. It exposes the imperfection of popular understanding of that principle. And it asserts the principle itself with luminous clarity and expansive power, giving the lie utterly to present-day claims that we began as a Christian nation. As Jefferson tells us, "a great majority" rejected an amendment to add "Jesus Christ, the holy author of our religion," to the landmark law, giving "proof that they meant to comprehend, within the mantle of its protection, the Jew and the Gentile, the Christian and the Mahometan, the Hindoo, and infidel of every denomination."

Or take the tantalizing glimpses the autobiography affords us of the astonishing insignificance of our earliest institutions of national governance, the Continental and Confederation Congresses. Jefferson himself quit the Congress within three months of drafting the Declaration of Independence for it, because he was elected in the interim to the Virginia House of Burgesses and "thought [he] could be of more use" there. Indeed, he would never have been in the Congress in the first place had others not shared his sentiments. Peyton Randolph was the most important politician in Virginia. He was speaker of the House of

Burgesses and president of the convention that selected delegates to the Continental Congress. As the
leader of the leading colony of the thirteen in incipi-
ent rebellion against Great Britain, he was chosen
chair of the Congress itself. But for him and his fellow
Virginians, resolving provincial conflicts with the royal
governor took precedence over guiding America at the
climax of the imperial crisis. As the break with Britain
impended, the proven leader, Randolph, returned to
tend to local affairs, while an untried young man, thir-
ty-two-year-old Jefferson, went off to serve the nation
in his place. Had Randolph and the rest of the Virginia
planters not put their priority on Williamsburg rather
than Philadelphia, Jefferson's mighty pen would never
have been at the disposal of the Revolution at the
hour of its most urgent rhetorical need.

Or take the autobiography's account of the adoption
of the Declaration of Independence itself. Jefferson
tells us almost nothing of his drafting of the document
that is, to this day, our iconic American scripture. "The
committee for drawing the declaration of Independence desired me to do it. It was accordingly done."
Not another word. But he provides us a stirring story
of the politicking that preceded the fateful vote of
July 4 and reminds us vividly of what a near thing it
was. To the second week of June, six of the thirteen
colonies were so reluctant to support rebellion that "it
was thought prudent to wait a while for them, and to
postpone the final decision to July 1." Even on July 1,
when the Congress "resumed," there were still just
nine colonies for independence. They were a majori-

ty, but they could never have sustained a revolution, especially since three of the four holdouts were New York, Pennsylvania, and Delaware. Without those middle colonies, the Revolution would have been riven into two revolutions, one in New England, the other in the South, and the southern one would itself have been riven by the defection of South Carolina. Great Britain would have made short work of both. Jefferson's laconic narrative of the maneuvers by which, in a few final hours, the four dissident colonies were brought round to revolution rebukes evocatively our schoolbook triumphalism. It reminds us that, from first to last, American independence hung by a thread.

Jefferson and all the Founding Fathers lived in a world of contingency we can scarcely conceive. And the autobiography intimates it again and again, so that we begin to see. Late in 1782, for example, he was made a minister plenipotentiary for negotiating the peace with Great Britain. He never sailed because his ship sat icebound in Baltimore for two months. The following year, he was elected a representative to Congress. He made the long, arduous journey from Charlottesville to the national capital in Trenton, New Jersey, and took his seat the day after he arrived, "on which day Congress adjourned to meet at Annapolis," the new capital, three weeks later. When the representatives finally reconvened in Annapolis, they discovered that there were only seven states in attendance and "no hope of our soon having nine," the minimum number requisite to ratification of the peace treaty, which was due to expire if not approved in two months. When such rampant absenteeism drove the Congress to give up sitting in permanent session and the representatives realized that their adjournments left the new nation with no government at all in the intermissions, they created a Committee of the States to remain in session during Congressional recesses. But as Jefferson wryly noted, the members of the committee "quarreled very soon, split into two parties, abandoned their post and left the government without any visible head until the next meeting in Congress."

The equanimity with which Jefferson met such misadventures exhibits his experimental, adventuring spirit. His extensive exposition of his plans for public education displays the ambiguities of his notions of the public weal, and so too, even more, does his repeated recurrence to his perplexities about race and slavery. A man probably cannot write 160-some pages about himself without revealing himself in some measure. Despite Jefferson's design, perhaps, his autobiography is a window on his psyche.

Consider the episode on which the memoir concludes, his visit to Franklin as the Philadelphian lay "on the bed of sickness from which he never rose." The two men talk of mutual friends in Paris and the parts they played in the revolution there. Then Jefferson congratulates Franklin on the report that the old man was writing "the history of his own life." Franklin replies by pressing upon Jefferson some of his own writing. Jefferson pledges to read it and return it. Franklin instructs him instead to "keep it." Later—too late, after he turns it over to Franklin's literary executor—Jefferson comes to believe "that Dr. Franklin had meant it as a confidential deposit in my hands, and that I had done wrong in parting from it." It is not hard to imagine that Jefferson saw in that gift a passing of the mantle from a Founding Father he admired immensely to a younger man who might also be a Father to his country.

So the puzzle persists. Why, with all that it has to offer, has Jefferson's autobiography been sunk in veritable oblivion for almost two hundred years?

Let us address that question by beginning at the beginning. Jefferson opens his memoir with a few perfunctory pages about his ancestry and his education. There was nothing original in this introduction. It followed a pattern set by others and certainly set for American autobiography by Franklin. But its lack of originality in this regard was hardly a fatal flaw. A generation later, P. T. Barnum's reminiscences would be far more derivative from Franklin's, yet Barnum's memoir would be the best-selling American autobiography of the nineteenth century.

Nonetheless, there may be a clue that is pertinent to our conundrum in the brevity of Jefferson's discussion of his family and his schooling.

Even at the outset, Franklin was more forthcoming about his family than the Virginian ever was, and through the remainder of his recollections Franklin recurred to his kin revealingly. Jefferson was done with his family before he was done with his second paragraph on the subject. Though he must have had things to say about his father, his mother, and his seven siblings, he kept them to himself. Though he must have had thoughts about the death of his father when he was still but a boy, and about the death of his mother in the very year he drafted the Declaration, he said nothing about either loss. Though he became the ward of his father's fabulously rich partner in western land-speculating, he wrote not a word about the transition or about his guardian.

Similarly, Franklin returned repeatedly to the topic of his education. He marked his meager formal schooling, intimated his anguish at his father's inability to send him to Harvard, and, in a succession of telling anecdotes, traced his subsequent efforts to teach himself what Harvard would not have taught him anyway. Jefferson devoted less than one long paragraph to his formal studies. His reluctance to confide family feelings and secrets may be understandable, but his omission of any more extensive treatment of his education is unfathomable.

Jefferson had a passion for learning. It was evident in his youth, throughout his life, and even in his death. He asked that three of his accomplishments be inscribed on his gravestone, and one of the three was the founding of the University of Virginia. He was a brilliant and precocious student from the first. He started school when he was four or five, began Latin school at nine, and entered the College of William and Mary at seventeen. Sons of the southern gentry attended William and Mary as a sort of finishing school. They rarely spent more than a year there, and they aimed to improve their manners more than their minds. Mostly they met other sons of the southern gentry whom it would be to their advantage to know later in life. Though the college was established in 1693, no one ever actually completed its four-year course of study and graduated with an earned degree in the first three-quarters of a century of its existence. Jefferson did not stay for four years either, but he did stay for two, and he was immensely serious about his studies. His professors mattered to him. He kept company with them more than with his dissipated fellow students while he was in residence in Williamsburg. And he only quit the college to commence an even more extended study with George Wythe, the man he called his "beloved Mentor." His years with Wythe must have been the most intellectually intense tutorial in American history.

Yet Jefferson allowed just three or four sentences to that tutorial, before passing on to politics. The inescapable inference is that he did not have the autobiographical impulse. He had to be "pressed" to write his memoir at all, though he never had to be pressed to write otherwise. Over the course of his career, he wrote more than 19,000 letters that survive (and unnumbered others that don't). Writing was, as much as anything, what he did in his life. Though he wrote incessantly, he had no lust to look back or to write about himself. And he certainly felt no urgency about taking up the task, no sense that time's winged chariot was hurrying near. He was deep into an advanced old age—long past the point when most men of his day died—when he got around to it.

Submitting at last to the importunities of others, he gave them the memoir they pressed him to produce. But we must not misunderstand. He did not write so singlemindedly about politics in petulant resistance to their desire for a more intimate or personal confession. He wrote about public life because he was a public man. He believed the republican writers he studied with George Wythe. He took to heart their insistence that citizenship was the highest calling a man could follow.

He said, again and again, that he was weary of civic service and longed to retreat to the pleasures of privacy at Monticello. But he had no great gift for intimacy or domesticity. He crowded his commonplace book with passages of acrid misogyny. He failed at his first proposal of marriage and did not offer again for eight years. He then married a wealthy widow, whom he called a spinster on the marriage license bond before he caught his slip and corrected it. His role in the Revolution kept him from home frequently during the decade she was his wife, and he never remarried after her death. He was a peremptory and platitudinous father to two daughters who survived infancy. And he denied utterly the five slave children he fathered with his longtime slave mistress Sally Hemings, as he denied Sally Hemings herself utterly.

Jefferson was simply not cut out for autobiography, or for the introspection and self-absorption it entails. Just seventy pages into this memoir, he confessed that he was "tired of talking about myself."

His was a temper immersed in the immediate. His genius was most manifest in the cut and thrust of conflict. His creativity was most evident when he was confronted with pressing problems. Even his inventiveness appeared in the little ingenuities that abound at Monticello. Though he was abreast of eighteenth-century science, he made no fundamental contributions to it, like Franklin's assimilation of electricity to the Newtonian paradigm. Though he had a mechanical gift, he left no lasting legacies to technology, like Franklin's lightning rod or bifocals. Though he was incorrigibly inquisitive, he did not make the discoveries that confer a minor immortality on lesser men, like Franklin's charting of the Gulf Stream. Where Franklin was sedentary, Jefferson was a man in motion. It was no accident that he was a superb horseman. He was at ease with philosophes, but he was not at his best in cool contemplation. He had his finest ideas and achieved his finest expression of them in the crucible of controversy. His mind worked best when he had to respond to crisis or rise to a rhetorical occasion. He was in his element looking to the future, ill at ease looking to the past.

Alas.

We have his words, wrought in the heat of battle, and we steer by them still. But we have nothing, here, to elaborate or explicate them. We have no hint, in this autobiography, how he came by the convictions they enunciate so eloquently.

"It does me no injury for my neighbor to say there are twenty gods or no god. It neither picks my pocket nor breaks my leg." How did Jefferson arrive at such a sublime acceptance of other religions and of irreligion? "You must . . . neither believe nor reject anything because other persons . . . have rejected or believed it. Your own reason is the only oracle given to you by heaven." How did he set aside the faith of his fathers and friends and put his trust solely in his own reason? How did he get clear of the established church of Virginia and of Protestant Christianity more broadly? How did he substitute a "wall of separation" between church and state for the government-mandated religion on which he grew up?

This memoir opened a clear, wide window on the war that Jefferson and his allies waged to win Virginia's Statute for Religious Freedom. It gave posterity a richly revelatory account of that bitter struggle, which certainly lasted longer and was perhaps more acrimonious even than the Revolution itself. But in it Jefferson betrayed nothing of the seeds of his own command of that war. He imputed motives to others who fought on one side or another, about which he could have only guessed. He said not a word about the evolution of his own religious views, about which he was the ultimate and almost the only authority.

By contrast, Franklin marked telling milestones on the march of his religious thinking throughout his autobiography. He did not tremble to describe the depth of his detachment from the conventional beliefs and practice of his parents and of their Puritan neighbors in Boston. He confessed the heterodoxy and the blasphemousness of his early ideas and the cynicism and faithlessness of his later professions of outward propriety. We meet the man in Franklin, merely the politician in Jefferson.

If Franklin exceeded Jefferson in the radicalism of his religiosity—in his youthful denial of the distinction between good and evil and in his lifelong flirtation with notions of polytheism and reincarnation—Jefferson exceeded Franklin in the depth of his antipathy to authority. "I have sworn upon the altar of God, eternal hostility against every form of tyranny over the mind of man," he wrote to one friend. "The tree of liberty must be refreshed from time to time with the blood of patriots and tyrants," he told another. "A little rebellion, now and then, is a good thing, and as necessary in the political world as storms in the physical," he assured a third.

These were mighty words even if they were only words. But in fact they were much more. They informed Jefferson's actions. His was a career of courage in opposing the highest powers in the land. He assailed King George III in the Declaration. He opposed George Washington in launching the Democratic-Republican Party. He alienated his fellow planters in instigating disestablishment and instituting a regime of sweeping religious liberty. He repudiated the law of the new nation in promoting the Virginia and Kentucky resolutions. Indeed, he set himself against cultural tradition itself. "The earth belongs to the living," he insisted, and any deference of present to past was an illegitimate concession of governance to ancestors in their graves.

Where did that seething antipathy to power come from? Franklin wrote openly of his early conflicts with his father and with the constituted authorities of

Boston. Jefferson wrote not at all of his relationship with his father, or of his feelings on losing his father when still just fourteen, or of his experience with his appointed guardian through the rest of his minority.

Americans may be as instinctively anti-authoritarian as any people on the planet. Jefferson was the most searing, soaring, searching voice of that animus against authority that we have ever had. How did he achieve that voice, at once so passionate and so measured? How did he keep his heart in such exquisite equipoise with his head? How did he arrive at such audacity and such assurance, to give utterance to our deepest dreams? Could there be questions more interesting to American readers? And could there be an autobiography more obtuse than this one to those questions? Jefferson did not even seem to suspect that his audience might be interested in asking them. He showed no slightest interest of his own in addressing them.

It is inconceivable that Jefferson was so unconcerned with what moved men. He was, after all, the greatest politician in our history. He could not have been the builder of our most consummately triumphant party organization if he had ignored what men wanted. He could not have been our president most masterful in handling Congress if he had been heedless of why they wanted what they wanted.

But he did not write as he ruled. In his recollections he displayed a disingenuous indifference to men's inner drives. He neither acknowledged nor explored his own, and he did not often impute any to those around him. Instead, he indulged in a bloodless democratic fantasy. At almost every decisive juncture, he explained developments by a disembodied movement of "the mind" of "the times."

In 1773, when a cadre of rebellious young Burgesses led by Jefferson and Patrick Henry pushed to organize inter-colonial committees of correspondence, the "old and leading members" of the assembly were not "up to the point of forwardness and zeal which the times required." In 1775, when independence was at hand, the deputies who hesitated were "not yet up to the mark of the times."

Jefferson's delusory democracy posited a unified "people" and an evolutionary ripening of "the public mind." It did not matter to him, in his memoirs, that Virginia had in fact harbored large numbers of loyalists and multitudes who did their damnedest to remain neutral. On the day appointed for election of delegates to the first Continental Congress, "the people met generally, with anxiety and alarm in their countenances, and the effect of the day through the whole colony was like a shock of electricity, arousing every man and placing him erect and solidly on his center."

It did not matter to him that many elected representatives in the second Congress held back from declaring independence, on the instructions of the voters who sent them. The will of "the people" could run contrary to the instructions they had voted. "The voice of the representatives" was "not always consonant with the voice of the people."

It did not even matter to him that overt opposition was rampant, or that he had no idea what he was talking about. At the call for a constitutional convention in 1787, "the people . . . agreed with one voice" to attempt a new compact to remedy the "incompetence" of the Articles of Confederation. This was sheerest nonsense. Popular opinion on the work of the Philadelphia convention was wildly divided. A majority of voters actually voted against the Constitution when it was submitted to them for ratification. And in any case Jefferson was not there to take the temperature of the electorate. He was an ocean away, in France, at the time. His account of the campaign for the new Constitution had nothing to do with reality but much to do with the cast of his mind. It expressed his impassioned yearning for an undifferentiated "people" devoted to the common good.

And yet he knew better. The people he idealized might unite now and then, for the public weal, but that was not their natural bent. "The pressure of an external enemy" had "hooped us together" in the war for independence, but once the war was over and "peace and safety were restored," such virtuous citizenship ceased. "Every man" looked to his own "profitable occupation." Jefferson was painfully aware that self-interest was the default position in American life.

He strained mightily against that awareness. He let his hopes get the best of his fears. He gave in to wishful thinking. In his first inaugural address, he proclaimed America "the strongest government on earth," despite the fact that its army was a pathetic thing and its navy nearly nonexistent. It was strong, he said, because "every man" would "fly" to defend that government if it called. (A few years later, when he called on his countrymen to uphold his embargo on commerce with Britain, he discovered the fatuousness of that faith.)

He exercised his imagination in fanciful schemes to divide Virginia's counties into much smaller jurisdictions he called wards. He understood full well that his wards would, by virtue of their size, be more homogeneous and thus more likely to trample the rights of deviants or to drive them away. Such tyranny of the majority was a risk he was ready to run, if it would keep people engaged in the republic, the "res publica," the public thing.

Jefferson celebrated the free individual, but he put no priority on free enterprise. He hoped that Americans would use their freedom as he had, for public life. He knew, long before Tocqueville spelled it out, that the citizens of a republic had to be "on the alert." They could lose their freedom if they did not guard the government that guarded it.

All his life, Jefferson was an advocate of small government. But he did not dread central government as modern conservatives do, as a check on the prerogatives of the private sector. On the contrary, he sought to scale down government as a means to preserve its power, keeping it close to the people and the people close to it. His priority was always on the public welfare more than personal fame or fortune. As he said in this memoir, the safety of the republic is "the first and supreme law."

Like Jefferson, Franklin felt the pull of the personal. Like Jefferson, Franklin fought it. But Franklin caught the wave of American life more presciently than Jefferson. Insisting as he did that there are "natural" claims that "precede political ones, and cannot be extinguished by them," Franklin set himself against privatism from within privatism, affirming benevolence as a better way to pursue happiness.

Jefferson's republican priorities were already out of fashion when he wrote his autobiography. They have been out of fashion ever since. He recognized as much at the time, and his recognition informs his recollections.

In the very year in which he put them to paper, he wrote to a friend, "I know no safe depository of the ultimate powers of the society but the people themselves; and if we think them not enlightened enough to exercise their control with a wholesome discretion, the remedy is not to take it from them but to inform their discretion." He still knew the tune. He just had not, any longer, the energy to dance to it.

His autobiography was an evocation of a golden age, a brief moment when men were "hooped together" in a common cause for the common good. It was not a summons to preserve that moment and that spirit of '76, because they were past, and Jefferson knew that they were past. It was not a clarion call to revive them, because he despaired of their revival.

This autobiography may be the most despairing thing that Jefferson ever wrote. Its odd inertness reflected his awareness that he was out of touch with "the times." Its halfheartedness expressed his abandonment of the endeavor that had informed his life, to educate the democracy. His account of the Revolutionary era was not intended as a trumpet blast. It was neither a call to battle nor an invitation to renewal. It was a more muted and somber thing, almost a taps, as if at least to have the reality of his outmoded values on the record, as if at least to insist that America had not always been as it was all too clearly going to be.

Americans could scarcely hear what he was saying when he said it in 1820, or when it was occasionally put before them in later years. Perhaps we cannot hear it now. We are surely more self-absorbed now, and less concerned for the commons, than even the despondent Jefferson of 1820 could have conceived. But there are signs that we begin to sicken of our amuck individualism. It is possible that, at this crisis of citizenship, in our hour of need, we are ready at last to listen.

CHIEF EVENTS IN JEFFERSON'S LIFE

FROM HIS BIRTH IN 1743 TO HIS DEATH IN 1826

1743.—April 2 [or 13]		Born at Shadwell, Albemarle Co., Va.
1748.		Attends English School at Tuckahoe.
1752.		Attends Latin School at Douglas.
1757.—August 17.		Death of his father, Peter Jefferson.
		Attends Murray School.
1760.—March 25.		Enters William and Mary College.
1762.—April 25.		Graduates from William and Mary.
		Enters law office of George Wythe.
1764.		At Williamsburg.
1766.		Journeys to Annapolis, Philadelphia, and New York.
1767.		Admitted to the bar from Shadwell.
1769.		Elected a Burgess from Shadwell.
	May 8.	Attends House of Burgesses.
		At Williamsburg.
	9.	Drafts resolutions in reply to Botetourt.
	17.	House of Burgesses dissolved.
		Signs Non-importation Association.
1770.—Feb. 1.		House and library at Shadwell burned.
		Argues case of Howell v. Netherland.
	May 11.	Attends House of Burgesses.
1771.		At Monticello.
	March 14.	Attends County Court at Albemarle.
	19.	Attends County Court at Augusta.
	April 10.	Attends County Court at Williamsburg.
	June 1.	At Monticello.
	11.	Attends Court at Oyer & Terminer at Williamsburg.
	October 10.	Argues case of Godwin et al v. Lunan.
	December 10.	Attends Court of Oyer & Terminer at Williamsburg.
1772.—Jan. 1.		Marries Martha (Waylies) Skelton.
	Sept. 27.	Birth of first daughter, Martha.

1773.—March 4.	Attends House of Burgesses at Williamsburg.
12.	Attends Committee of Correspondence.
October 14.	Appointed Surveyor of Albemarle County.
1774.—April 3.	Birth of second daughter, Jane Randolph.
May 9.	Attends House of Burgesses.
July 26.	Drafts the resolutions of Albemarle Co. Writes "A Summary View."
1775.—Jan. 5.	Elected member of Albemarle Committee of Safety.
March 20.	Attends Convention at Richmond.
23.	Placed on Committee for Defense of Colony.
27.	Elected deputy delegate to the Continental Congress.
June 2.	On Committee to Draft Address to the Governor.
10.	Prepares address to Governor Dunmore.
21.	Attends Continental Congress at Philadelphia. Placed on Committee to Draft Declaration on Army and Prepares draft.
July 31.	Reports from Committee Draft and Reply to Lord North's Motion.
August 9.	Attends at Richmond Convention of Va.
11.	Reëlected member of Continental Congress.
16.	Placed on Committee on Defense.
October 2.	Attends at Philadelphia session of Continental Congress.
Nov. 16.	Placed on Committee on Massachusetts Papers.
23.	Placed on Committee on Currency.
24.	Placed on Committee on Condition of N. C.
Dec. 15.	Prepares rules for Committee of Congress.
22.	Placed on Committee on Business of Congress.
1776.—March 31.	Death of Jefferson's mother.
May 21.	Draft of Report of Congressional Committee on Letters. Placed on Committee to Address Foreign Mercenaries.
June 2.	Drafts Constitution for Va.
5.	Placed on Committee for Procuring News and Supplies.
10.	On Committee to Prepare Rules for Congress.
11.	On Committee to Prepare Declaration of Independence.
17.	Draft Report of such Committee.
20.	Reëlected member of Congress. Draft Report on Canada.
28.	Reports draft of Declaration of Independence.

1776.—July 4.	Adopted Declaration.
5.	Placed on Committee to Plan Seal for U. S.
6.	Placed on Committee on Indian Affairs.
Aug. 9.	Placed on Committee to Encourage Hessians to Desert.
Sept. 26.	Elected Commissioner of France.
Oct. 11.	Placed on Committee on Propositions and Grievances.
	On Committee on Privileges and Elections.
15.	On Committee to Draft Infantry Bill.
16.	On Committee to Draft Punishment Bill.
21.	On Committee to Draft Bill to Remove Seat of Government and on Committee to Draft Naturalization Bill.
25.	On Committee to Draft Congress Bill.
28.	On Committee to Draft Bill to Define Treason.
Nov. 6.	Chosen one of five to revise the laws.
7.	On Committee to Draft Copper-Coinage Bill.
11.	Introduces Bill to Remove Capital.
1777.—Dec. 13.	On Committee to Draft Tax Bill.
	On Committee to Draft Salary Bill.
27.	On Committee to Amend Small-Pox Bill.
1778.—Jan. 20.	On Committee to Draft Chancery Court Bill.
May 18.	On Committee to Draft Bill for Recovery of Debts.
June 10.	Leaves Williamsburg.
Aug. 1.	Third daughter born (Mary Jefferson).
1779.—Jan. 22.	At Williamsburg.
Nov. 30.	Issues Proclamation Laying Embargo.
1780.—June 1.	Reëlected Governor of Virginia.
Nov. 3.	Birth of fourth daughter.
Dec. 31.	Receives news of Leslie's Invasion.
1781.—Jan. 2.	Orders out militia.
Feb. 5.	Issues Proclamation Concerning Foreigners.
April 15.	Death of son.
June 1.	Resigns Governorship.
14.	Appointed by Congress Peace Commissioner, which appointment he declines.
July.	Begins preparation of Notes on Virginia.
Nov. 30.	Elected delegate to Continental Congress.
Dec. 10.	Placed on Committee on Finance.
19.	Declines appointment for Congress.
1782.—Sept.	Birth of youngest daughter, Lucy Elizabeth.
6.	Death of wife.
Nov. 12.	Appointed Peace Commissioner to Europe.
Dec. 19.	Arrives at Philadelphia.

1783.—Feb. 14.		Departure to Europe suspended.
	April 1.	Congress withdraws appointment.
	June 6.	Elected delegate to Congress.
	10.	Drafts Constitution for Virginia.
	Nov. 4.	Congress adjourns to Annapolis.
	Dec. 16.	Reports on definitive treaty.
	22.	Reports on ceremonial for Washington.
	27.	Reports on ratification of treaty.
1784.—Jan. 14.		Reports Proclamation of British Treaty.
	March 1.	Reports on Government for Western Territory.
	5.	Reports on Indiana.
	12.	Elected Chairman of Congress.
	13.	Placed on Committee on Qualifications and on Foreign Letters.
	30.	Elected Chairman of Congress.
	April 5.	Prepares Notes on a Money Unit.
	13.	Drafts resolution concerning seat of Government.
	May 3.	Reports ordinance for Western lands.
	23.	Report on Western Territory considered and adopted.
	July 5.	Sails from Boston on ship *Ceres*.
	Aug. 6.	Reaches Paris.
	10.	At Passy, conferring with Franklin.
	Sept.13.	Sends the first Notes on Virginia.
	15.	At Versailles, with Commissioners, to meet Vergennes.
	16.	The Commissioners meet the British Ministers.
1785.—March 10.		Elected by Congress Minister to France.
	May 11.	Completes Notes on Virginia.
	July 28.	Signs treaty with Prussia.
	November.	Death in Virginia of the youngest daughter, Lucy Elizabeth.
1786.—March 5.		Leaves Paris for London.
	22.	Presented at Windsor to the King.
	23.	Negotiates treaty with Portugal.
	26.	Prepares with Adams *projet* of treaty with Great Britain.
	May 23.	Plans treaty against Barbary States.
	Oct. 22.	Prepares map of Virginia.
	Dec. 16.	Act of Religious Freedom passed by the Virginia Assembly.
	26.	Publication of French version of Notes on Virginia.

1787.—Jan. 4.		Makes proposition to British creditors.
	April, May, June.	Tour through France.
	Sept.	Finishes map of Virginia.
	Dec.	Publication in England of "Notes on Virginia."
1788.—Feb. 4.		Leaves Paris.
	11.	Declines membership in Society for Abolition of Slave Trade.
	April	Journey to Germany.
	June 20.	Receives from Harvard degree of LL.D.
1789.—May 8.		Attends the opening at Versailles of the States-General.
	June 3.	Prepares charter for France.
	July 17.	Views ruins of Bastille.
	Sept. 25.	Jefferson nominated for Secretary of State.
	26.	Confirmed by Senate.
	Oct.	Sails for America on the *Montgomery*.
1790.—Feb. 14.		Accepts Secretaryship of State.
	28.	Arranges with Dutch bankers for a loan.
		Marriage of Jefferson's daughter Martha to Thomas Mann Randolph.
	March 29.	Takes residence in Maiden Lane, New York City.
		Elected member of American Arts and Sciences.
	June 7.	Arranges with Hamilton the Assumption and Capital Compromise.
	July 4.	Reports on coinage, weights, and measures.
	Aug. 22.	Drafts Considerations on Navigation of Mississippi.
	26.	Opinion on Foreign Debt.
	28.	Opinion on course toward Britain and Spain.
	Nov. 21.	Takes residence in Philadelphia.
	Dec. 8.	Draft of paragraph for President's Message.
1791.		Prepares Report on Fisheries.
		Reports on Algerian Prisoners.
	Feb. 14.	Draft of President's Message on British Negotiations.
	15.	Opinion on National Bank.
	28.	Offers Freneau a place.
	May.	Endorses Paine's *Rights of Man*.
		Arranges with Freneau for the publication of a paper.
	July.	Endeavors to have Thomas Paine appointed postmaster.
1792.		Draft of President's Message on Diplomatic Nominations.

1792.—Feb. 28.	Announces to President intention to leave office.
May 23.	Writes to Washington of intended resignation.
Sept. 9.	Writes to President in defense of conduct.
1793.—Jan.	Reconsiders resignation.
Feb. 7.	Paper on maladministration (by Hamilton) of the Treasury.
April 8.	Genet lands at Charleston.
18.	Drafts Cabinet Opinion on Proclamation and French Minister.
May 8.	Opposes Hamilton's circular to collectors.
July 5.	Receives call from Genet.
8.	Dissents from Cabinet Opinion on *Little Sarah*.
Aug. 2.	Recall of Genet decided upon by the Cabinet.
31.	Drafts Cabinet Opinion on Privateers and Prizes.
Nov. 16.	Borrows money.
23.	Drafts Message to the President.
Dec. 31.	Resigns Secretaryship of State.
1794.—Sept.	Offer of foreign mission.
1795.—Dec.	Invents mould-board for plough.
1796.—May 12.	Executes mortgage on his home.
Nov. 4.	Elected Vice-President.
1797.—Jan.	Elected President to Philosophical Society.
1797.—Jan. 25.	Letter written to Mazzei (in 1796) printed in Paris.
March 4.	Sworn in as Vice-President.
5.	Offer of French Mission.
May 14.	Mazzei letter printed in America.
Oct. 13.	Marriage of Maria Jefferson to John Waylies Eppes.
1798.—Feb. 19.	X Y Z Message.
July 6.	Passage of the Alien Bill.
14.	Passage of the Sedition Bill.
Oct.	Draft of the Kentucky Resolutions.
Nov. 14.	Kentucky Legislature adopts resolutions.
15.	Refuses Virginia Resolutions of Madison.
1800.—Jan. 18.	Drafts plan for the University of Va.
Feb.	Prepares Parliamentary Manual.
May.	Republican Caucus nominates Jefferson and Burr.
June.	Removal of the capital to Washington.
Dec. 14.	Offers Secretaryship of Navy to Livingston.
1801.—Feb. 17.	Election of Jefferson as President.
18.	Offers Secretaryship of War to Dearborn.
24.	Offers French Mission to Livingston.

1801.—Feb. 28.		Farewell speech to Senate.
	March 4.	Inauguration of Jefferson as President.
	5.	Nominates Madison, Dearborn, and Lincoln to Cabinet.
	9.	Cabinet remits fines under Sedition Law.
	18.	Offers Paine passage on public vessel.
	May 14.	Appoints Gallatin Secretary of Treasury.
	15.	Cabinet discusses Barbary War.
		Squadron ordered to Mediterranean.
	July 15.	Appoints Robert Smith Secretary of Navy.
	Nov. 28.	Appoints Granger Postmaster-General.
1803.—Jan. 11.		Nominates Monroe Joint Minister to France.
	18.	Sends secret message on Lewis and Clark Expedition.
	April.	Prepares estimate of Christ.
	11.	Talleyrand offers to sell Louisiana.
	May 2.	Louisiana treaty signed at Paris.
	July.	Frames Louisiana Amendment to the Constitution.
	24.	Appoints Monroe Minister to Great Britain.
	Oct. 20.	Louisiana treaty ratified by Senate.
1804.—Jan. 8.		Offers Monroe Governorship of Louisiana.
	Feb. 18.	Approves act organizing Louisiana and Orleans.
	April 17.	Death of daughter Mary.
	May 26.	Appoints Monroe Minister to Spain.
	Nov.	Reëlected President of United States.
	19.	Nominates Bowdoin Minister to Spain.
1805.—March 2.		Appoints Robert Smith Attorney-General.
		Appoints Jacob Crowninshield Secretary of Navy.
	4.	Inaugurated as President.
	August.	Prepares Note on Conduct 1780–1.
		Suggests alliance with Great Britain.
	Dec. 20.	Nominates John Breckenridge Attorney-General
1806.—Feb. 24.		Aids Barlow to Draft Bill for a National University.
	28.	Nominated Bowdoin and Armstrong Joint Commissioners to Spain.
	April 19.	Writes letter to Alexander of Russia.
		Nominates Monroe and Pinkney Joint Commissioners.
	Oct. 25.	Cabinet decision on Burr.
	Nov. 8.	Orders to Wilkinson, *in re* Burr.
1807.—Jan. 28.		Sends additional message to Burr.
	31.	Sends message to Cumberland Road.

1807.—Feb. 22.		Cabinet Council on British negotiations.
	Feb. 28.	Writes to King of Holland.
	March 2.	Sends Bill to End Slave Trade.
	30.	Beginning of trial of Burr.
	June 22.	Capture of the *Chesapeake*.
	Sept. 1.	Proposes to seize the Floridas.
	11.	Acquittal of Burr.
	Nov. 11.	Great Britain extends Orders in Council.
	Dec. 22.	Signs Embargo Act.
1808.—Jan. 23.		Refuses to recommend Fast Day.
	Feb. 19.	Sends message on Cumberland Road.
	29.	Sends reply to New York Society of St. Tammany.
	April 19.	Issues Proclamation on Embargo.
1809.—Jan. 17.		Forced to borrow money.
	March 1.	Sends repeal of Embargo.
	4.	Sends reply to citizens of Washington.
		Close of Presidential term.
		Issues circular letter on Public Appointments.
1811.—Jan.		Urges seizures of the Floridas.
1812.—April 12.		Sends Wirt his recollections of Patrick Henry.
	Dec. 17.	Writes sketch of Meriwether Lewis.
1813.—July.		Sells Mazzei's property in Richmond and borrows purchase money.
1814.—Sept. 21.		Offers Library to Congress.
	Nov. 21.	Resigns presidency of American Philosophical Society.
1815.—Jan.		Congress passes Bill to Purchase Library.
		Completes scheme for the University of Va.
1816.—July 10.		Writes sketch of Peyton Randolph.
	Oct. 16.	Writes inscription for National Capitol.
1818.—Sept. 1.		Writes Anecdotes of Franklin.
1822.—May.		Writes answer to "A Native of Virginia."
1825.—Dec.		Drafts Protest for Virginia.
1826.—March 16.		Executes will.
	July 4.	**Death of Jefferson.**

The Autobiography of
Thomas Jefferson,

1743–1790

THE WRITINGS

OF

THOMAS JEFFERSON

AUTOBIOGRAPHY

1743–1790

1821. Jan, 6.

At the age of 77, I begin to make some memoranda and state some recollections of dates & facts concerning myself, for my own more ready reference & for the information of my family.

The tradition in my father's family was that their ancestor came to this country from Wales, and from near the mountain of Snowdon, the highest in Gr. Br. I noted once a case from Wales in the law reports where a person of our name was either pl. or def. and one of the same name was Secretary to the Virginia company.[1] These are the only instances in which I have met with the name in that country. I have found it in our early records, but the first particular information I have of any ancestor was

---

[1] No Jefferson was ever secretary of the Virginia Company, but John Jefferson was a member of the company. He came to Virginia in the *Bona Nova*, in 1619.

3

my grandfather who lived at the place in Chesterfield called Ozborne's and ownd. the lands afterwards the glebe of the parish.[1] He had three sons, Thomas who died young, Field who settled on the waters of Roanoke and left numerous descendants, and Peter my father, who settled on the lands I still own called Shadwell [2] adjoining my present residence. He was born Feb. 29, 1707/8, and intermarried 1739, with Jane Randolph, of the age of 19. daur of Isham Randolph one of the seven sons of that name & family settled at Dungeoness in Goochld. They trace their pedigree far back in England & Scotland, to which let every one ascribe the faith & merit he chooses.

My father's education had been quite neglected; but being of a strong mind, sound judgment and eager after information, he read much and improved himself insomuch that he was chosen with Joshua Fry, professor of Mathem. in W. & M. college to continue the boundary line between Virginia & N. Caroline which had been begun by Colo Byrd, and was afterwards employed with the same Mr. Fry to make the 1st map of Virginia [3] which had ever been made, that of Capt Smith being merely a conjectural sketch. They possessed excellent materials for so much of the country as is below the blue ridge; little being then known beyond that ridge. He was the

---

[1] This was Capt. Thomas Jefferson, son of Thomas and Mary (Branch) Jefferson, of Henrico Co. He married Mary Field.

[2] In Albemarle County. The house lot of 400 acres was purchased from William Randolph by "Henry Weatherbourne's biggest bowl of arrack punch."

[3] Engraved and printed on four sheets in London, in 1751, by Thomas Jeffreys. The name Shadwell which it contains is even then one of the most western of settlements.

3d or 4th settler of the part of the country in which
I live, which was about 1737. He died Aug. 17.
1757, leaving my mother a widow who lived till 1776,
with 6 daurs & 2. sons, myself the elder.[1] To my
younger brother he left his estate on James river
called Snowden after the supposed birth-place of the
family. To myself the lands on which I was born &
live. He placed me at the English school at 5. years
of age and at the Latin at 9. where I continued until
his death. My teacher Mr. Douglas[2] a clergyman
from Scotland was but a superficial Latinist, less instructed in Greek, but with the rudiments of these
languages he taught me French, and on the death of
my father I went to the revd. Mr. Maury[3] a correct
classical scholar, with whom I continued two years,
and then went to Wm. and Mary college, to wit in
the spring of 1760, where I continued 2. years. It
was my great good fortune, and what probably fixed

[1] In Colonel Peter Jefferson's Prayer Book in the handwriting of
Thomas Jefferson, are the following entries:

"	"BIRTHS	MARRIAGES	DEATHS
"Jane Jefferson	1740, June 17	———	1765 Oct 1
Mary	1741, Oct 1	1760 June 24	———
Thomas	1743, Apr 2	1772 Jan 1	———
Elizabeth	1744, Nov. 4	———	1773 Jan 1
Martha	1746, May 29	1765 July 20	———
Peter Field	1748, Oct 16	———	1748 Nov. 29
A son	1750, March 9	———	1750 Mar. 9
Lucy	1752, Oct 10	1769 Sept. 12	———
Anna Scott Randolph	1755, Oct 1	1788, October	———"

[2] The Rev. William Douglas, of St. James, Northam Parish, Gooch-
land.

[3] Rev. James Maury, of Fredericksville, Louisa Co., "an ingenious
young man, who tho' born of French parents, has lived with them in
this country of Virginia since he was a very young child. He has been
educated at our College."-- ˈ . . . . *Bishop of London*, 1742

the destinies of my life that Dr. Wm. Small of Scotland was then professor of Mathematics, a man profound in most of the useful branches of science, with a happy talent of communication correct and gentlemanly manners, & an enlarged & liberal mind. He, most happily for me, became soon attached to me & made me his daily companion when not engaged in the school; and from his conversation I got my first views of the expansion of science & of the system of things in which we are placed.   Fortunately the Philosophical chair became vacant soon after my arrival at college, and he was appointed to fill it per interim: and he was the first who ever gave in that college regular lectures in Ethics, Rhetoric & Belles lettres.   He returned to Europe in 1762, having previously filled up the measure of his goodness to me, by procuring for me, from his most intimate friend G. Wythe, a reception as a student of law, under his direction, and introduced me to the acquaintance and familiar table of Governor Fauquier, the ablest man who had ever filled that office. With him, and at his table, Dr. Small & Mr. Wythe, his amici omnium horarum, & myself, formed a partie quarree, & to the habitual conversations on these occasions I owed much instruction.   Mr. Wythe continued to be my faithful and beloved Mentor in youth, and my most affectionate friend through life. In 1767, he led me into the practice of the law at the bar of the General court, at which I continued until the revolution shut up the courts of justice. [For a sketch of the life & character of Mr. Wythe see my letter of Aug. 21 20 to Mr. John Saunderson]

In 1769, I became a member of the legislature by
the choice of the county in which I live, & continued
in that until it was closed by the revolution.   I
made one effort in that body for the permission of
the emancipation of slaves,[1] which was rejected:
and indeed, during the regal government, nothing
liberal could expect success.   Our minds were cir-
cumscribed within narrow limits by an habitual belief that it was our duty to be subordinate to the
mother country in all matters of government, to
direct all our labors in subservience to her interests,
and even to observe a bigoted intolerance for all
religions but hers.   The difficulties with our representatives were of habit and despair, not of reflection
& conviction.   Experience soon proved that they
could bring their minds to rights on the first summons of their attention.   But the king's council,
which acted as another house of legislature, held
their places at will & were in most humble obedience
to that will: the Governor too, who had a negative
on our laws held by the same tenure, & with still
greater devotedness to it: and last of all the Royal
negative closed the last door to every hope of
amelioration.

On the 1st of January, 1772 I was married to
Martha Skelton widow of Bathurst Skelton, &
daughter of John Wayles, then 23. years old.   Mr.
Wayles was a lawyer of much practice, to which he

[1] Under the act of 2d George II., no slave was to be set "free upon
any pretence whatsoever, except for some meritorious services, to be
adjudged and allowed by the Governor and Council."—*Acts of the
Assembly, 1769*.   No trace of this "effort" is recorded in the *Journal
of the House of Burgesses.*

was introduced more by his great industry, punctuality & practical readiness, than to eminence in the science of his profession.   He was a most agreeable companion, full of pleasantry & good humor, and welcomed in every society.   He acquired a handsome fortune, died in May, 1773, leaving three daughters, and the portion which came on that event to Mrs. Jefferson, after the debts should be paid, which were very considerable, was about equal to my own patrimony, and consequently doubled the ease of our circumstances.

When the famous Resolutions of 1765, against the Stamp-act, were proposed, I was yet a student of law in Wmsbg.   I attended the debate however at the door of the lobby of the H. of Burgesses, & heard the splendid display of Mr. Henry's talents as a popular orator.   They were great indeed; such as I have never heard from any other man.   He appeared to me to speak as Homer wrote.   Mr. Johnson, a lawyer & member from the Northern Neck, seconded the resolns, & by him the learning & the logic of the case were chiefly maintained.   My recollections of these transactions may be seen pa. 60, Wirt's life of P. H.,[1] to whom I furnished them.

In May,[2] 1769, a meeting of the General Assembly was called by the Govr., Ld. Botetourt.   I had then become a member; and to that meeting became known the joint resolutions & address of the Lords & Commons of 1768-9, on the proceedings in Massachusetts.   Counter-resolutions, & an address to the

[1] Patrick Henry.   *Cf. post*, sketch of Patrick Henry, under 1814.
[2] May 8th.

King, by the H. of Burgesses were agreed to with little opposition, & a spirit manifestly displayed of considering the cause of Massachusetts as a common one. The Governor dissolved us [1]: but we met the next day in the Apollo [2] of the Raleigh tavern, formed ourselves into a voluntary convention, drew up articles of association against the use of any merchandise imported from Gr. Britain, signed and recommended them to the people, repaired to our several counties, & were re elected without any other exception than of the very few who had declined assent to our proceedings.

Nothing of particular excitement occurring for a considerable time our countrymen seemed to fall into a state of insensibility to our situation. The duty on tea not yet repealed & the Declaratory act of a right in the British parl. to bind us by their laws in all cases whatsoever, still suspended over us. But a court of inquiry held in R. Island in 1762, with a power to send persons to England to be tried for offences committed here [3] was considered at our session of the spring of 1773. as demanding attention. Not thinking our old & leading members up to the point of forwardness & zeal which the times required, Mr. Henry, R. H. Lee, Francis L. Lee, Mr. Carr & myself agreed to meet in the evening in a private room of the Raleigh to consult on the state of things. There may have been a member or two more whom I

[1] May 16th.

[2] A public room sometimes called the "long room" in the tavern. There is a picture of it in *The Century Magazine* for November, 1875.

[3] This was the famous "Gaspee" inquiry, the date being a slip for 1772.

do not recollect. We were all sensible that the most
urgent of all measures was that of coming to an
understanding with all the other colonies to consider
the British claims as a common cause to all, & to
produce an unity of action: and for this purpose that
a commee of correspondce in each colony would
be the best instrument for intercommunication: and
that their first measure would probably be to propose a meeting of deputies from every colony at
some central place, who should be charged with the
direction of the measures which should be taken by
all. We therefore drew up the resolutions which
may be seen in Wirt pa 87. The consulting members
proposed to me to move them, but I urged that it
should be done by Mr. Carr,[1] my friend & brother in
law, then a new member to whom I wished an opportunity should be given of making known to the
house his great worth & talents. It was so agreed;
he moved them, they were agreed to nem. con. and a
commee of correspondence appointed of whom Peyton Randolph, the Speaker, was chairman. The
Govr. (then Ld. Dunmore) dissolved us, but the
commee met the next day, prepared a circular letter
to the Speakers of the other colonies, inclosing to
each a copy of the resolns and left it in charge with
their chairman to forward them by expresses.

The origination of these commees of correspondence between the colonies has been since claimed for
Massachusetts, and Marshall II. 151, has given into
this error, altho' the very note of his appendix to
which he refers, shows that their establmt was con-

---

[1] Dabney Carr. He married Martha Jefferson.

fined to their own towns.   This matter will be seen
clearly stated in a letter of Samuel Adams Wells to
me of Apr. 2, 1819, and my answer of May 12.   I
was corrected by the letter of Mr. Wells in the information I had given Mr. Wirt, as stated in his note,
pa. 87, that the messengers of Massach. & Virga
crossed each other on the way bearing similar propositions, for Mr. Wells shows that Mass. did not
adopt the measure but on the receipt of our proposn
delivered at their next session.   Their message
therefore which passed ours, must have related to
something else, for I well remember P. Randolph's
informing me of the crossing of our messengers.

The next event which excited our sympathies for
Massachusets was the Boston port bill, by which
that port was to be shut up on the 1st of June, 1774.
This arrived while we were in session in the spring of
that year.   The lead in the house on these subjects
being no longer left to the old members, Mr. Henry,
R. H. Lee, Fr. L. Lee, 3. or 4. other members, whom
I do not recollect, and myself, agreeing that we must
boldly take an unequivocal stand in the line with
Massachusetts, determined to meet and consult on
the proper measures in the council chamber, for the
benefit of the library in that room.   We were under
conviction of the necessity of arousing our people
from the lethargy into which they had fallen as to
passing events; and thought that the appointment
of a day of general fasting & prayer would be
most likely to call up & alarm their attention.[1]   No

---

[1] "Mr. Jefferson and Charles Lee may be said to have originated a
fast to electrify the people from the pulpit. . . . . Those gentlemen,

example of such a solemnity had existed since the days of our distresses in the war of 55. since which a new generation had grown up. With the help therefore of Rushworth, whom we rummaged over for the revolutionary precedents & forms of the Puritans of that day, preserved by him, we cooked up a resolution, somewhat modernizing their phrases, for appointing the 1st day of June, on which the Port bill was to commence, for a day of fasting, humiliation & prayer, to implore heaven to avert from us the evils of civil war, to inspire us with firmness in support of our rights, and to turn the hearts of the King & parliament to moderation & justice.[1] To give greater emphasis to our proposition, we agreed to wait the next morning on Mr. Nicholas,[2] whose grave & religious character was more in unison with the tone of our resolution and to solicit him to move it. We accordingly went to him in the morning. He moved it the same day; the 1st of June was proposed and it passed without opposition.[3] The Governor dis-

knowing that Robert Carter Nicholas, the chairman of the committee of religion, was no less zealous than themselves against the attempt to starve thousands of American people into a subservience to the ministry, easily persuaded him to put forth the strength of his character, on an occasion which he thought to be pious, and move a fast, to be observed on the first day of June.—Edmund Randolph's (MS.) *History of Virginia*, p. 24.

  [1] Printed in Force's *Archives*, 4th, 1, 350.
  [2] Robert Carter Nicholas.
  [3] "It (the fast) was spoke of by some as a Schem calculated to *inflame* and excite an *enthusiastic* zeal in the Minds of the People under a Cloak of Religion, than which nothing could be more *calumnious* and *unjust* . . . The Resolution was not *Smuggled*, but proposed in a very *full* House, not above one Dissentient appearing amongst near an hundred members."—R. C. Nicholas' *Considerations on the Present State of Virginia Examined*, p. 40.

solved us as usual. We retired to the Apollo as before, agreed to an association,[1] and instructed the commee of correspdce to propose to the corresponding commees of the other colonies to appoint deputies to meet in Congress at such place, *annually*, as should be convenient to direct, from time to time, the measures required by the general interest: and we declared that an attack on any one colony should be considered as an attack on the whole. This was in May.[2] We further recommended to the several counties to elect deputies to meet at Wmsbg the 1st of Aug ensuing, to consider the state of the colony, & particularly to appoint delegates to a general Congress, should that measure be acceded to by the commees of correspdce generally.[3] It was acceded to, Philadelphia was appointed for the place, and the 5th of Sep. for the time of meeting. We returned home, and in our several counties invited the clergy to meet assemblies of the people on the 1st of June,[4] to perform the ceremonies of the day, & to address to them discourses suited to the occasion. The people met generally, with anxiety & alarm in their countenances, and the effect of the day thro' the whole colony was like a shock of electricity, arousing every man & placing him erect & solidly on his centre.

[1] Printed in Rind's *Virginia Gazette* for May 26, 1774. It was signed by eighty-nine members.

[2] May 27, 1774.

[3] This was in a separate resolution, adopted May 30th, by "all the members that were then in town." It was not to "elect deputies" but merely a reference of the consideration of important papers to such "late members of the House of Burgesses" who should then gather.

[4] By the original invitation, printed herein under June, 1774, it will be seen that the call was for June 23d, instead of the 1st.

They chose universally delegates for the convention. Being elected one for my own county I prepared a draught of instructions to be given to the delegates whom we should send to the Congress, and which I meant to propose at our meeting. In this I took the ground which, from the beginning I had thought the only one orthodox or tenable, which was that the relation between Gr. Br. and these colonies was exactly the same as that of England & Scotland after the accession of James & until the Union, and the same as her present relations with Hanover, having the same Executive chief but no other necessary political connection; and that our emigration from England to this country gave her no more rights over us, than the emigrations of the Danes and Saxons gave to the present authorities of the mother country over England. In this doctrine however I had never been able to get any one to agree with me but Mr. Wythe. He concurred in it from the first dawn of the question What was the political relation between us & England? Our other patriots Randolph, the Lees, Nicholas, Pendleton stopped at the half-way house of John Dickinson who admitted that England had a right to regulate our commerce, and to lay duties on it for the purposes of regulation, but not of raising revenue. But for this ground there was no foundation in compact, in any acknowledged principles of colonization, nor in reason: expatriation being a natural right, and acted on as such, by all nations, in all ages. I set out for Wmsbg some days before that appointed for our meeting, but was taken ill of a dysentery on the road, & unable to pro-

ceed. I sent on therefore to Wmsbg two copies of
my draught, the one under cover to Peyton Randolph, who I knew would be in the chair of the convention, the other to Patrick Henry. Whether Mr.
Henry disapproved the ground taken, or was too
lazy to read it (for he was the laziest man in reading
I ever knew) I never learned: but he communicated
it to nobody. Peyton Randolph informed the convention he had received such a paper from a member
prevented by sickness from offering it in his place,
and he laid it on the table for perusal. It was read
generally by the members, approved by many, but
thought too bold for the present state of things; but
they printed it in pamphlet form under the title of
A Summary view of the rights of British America.
It found its way to England, was taken up by the
opposition, interpolated a little by Mr. Burke so as
to make it answer opposition purposes, and in that
form ran rapidly thro' several editions.[1] This information I had from Parson Hurt,[2] who happened
at the time to be in London, whither he had gone to
receive clerical orders. And I was informed afterwards by Peyton Randolph that it had procured me
the honor of having my name inserted in a long list
of proscriptions enrolled in a bill of attainder commenced in one of the houses of parliament, but suppressed in embryo by the hasty step of events which
warned them to be a little cautious.[3] Montague,

---

[1] There are several errors in this statement, which are treated in the
note on the pamphlet. See *post*, 1774.

[2] Rev. John Hurt.

[3] It is hardly necessary to state that this so-called bill was a myth,
which had no basis in fact. But at the time when these leaders were

agent of the H. of Burgesses in England made extracts from the bill, copied the names, and sent them to Peyton Randolph. The names I think were about 20 which he repeated to me, but I recollect those only of Hancock, the two Adamses, Peyton Randolph himself, Patrick Henry, & myself.[1] The convention met on the 1st of Aug, renewed their association, appointed delegates to the Congress, gave them instructions very temperately & properly expressed, both as to style & matter; and they repaired to Philadelphia at the time appointed. The splendid proceedings of that Congress at their 1st session belong to general history, are known to every one, and need not therefore be noted here. They terminated their session on the 26th of Octob, to meet again on the 10th May ensuing. The convention at their ensuing session of Mar, '75,[2] approved of the proceedings of Congress, thanked their delegates and reappointed the same persons to represent the colony at the meeting to be held in May: and foreseeing the probability that Peyton Randolph their president and Speaker also of the H. of B. might be called off, they added me, in that event to the delegation.

Mr. Randolph was according to expectation obliged to leave the chair of Congress to attend the Gen. Assembly summoned by Ld. Dunmore to meet on the 1st day of June 1775. Ld. North's conciliatory

risking such a proscription, it was the current belief, both in England and America, that steps would be taken against them, and it is not strange that, in the absence of the proof to the contrary which we now possess, it was believed in.

[1] See Girardin's *History of Virginia*, Appendix No. 12, note.—*T. J.*

[2] March 27, 1775. See Force's *Archives*, 4th, 11, 172.

propositions, as they were called, had been received by the Governor and furnished the subject for which this assembly was convened. Mr. Randolph accordingly attended, and the tenor of these propositions being generally known, as having been addressed to all the governors, he was anxious that the answer of our assembly, likely to be the first,[1] should harmonize with what he knew to be the sentiments and wishes of the body he had recently left. He feared that Mr. Nicholas, whose mind was not yet up to the mark of the times, would undertake the answer, & therefore pressed me to prepare an answer. I did so, and with his aid carried it through the house with long and doubtful scruples from Mr. Nicholas and James Mercer, and a dash of cold water on it here & there, enfeebling it somewhat, but finally with unanimity or a vote approaching it.[2] This being passed, I repaired immediately to Philadelphia, and conveyed to Congress the first notice they had of it. It was entirely approved there. I took my seat with them on the 21st of June. On the 24th, a commee which had been appointed to prepare a declaration of the causes of taking up arms, brought in their report (drawn I believe by J. Rutledge) which not being liked they recommitted it on the 26th, and added Mr. Dickinson and myself to the committee. On the rising of the house, the commee having not yet met, I happened to find myself near Govr W. Livingston, and proposed to him to draw the paper.

[1] It had already been referred to the Congress by New Jersey, May 20th, 1775.
[2] See *post*, under June 12, 1775.

He excused himself and proposed that I should draw
it.   On my pressing him with urgency, "we are as
yet but new acquaintances, sir, said he, why are you
so earnest for my doing it?"   "Because, said I, I
have been informed that you drew the Address to
the people of Gr. Britain, a production certainly of
the finest pen in America."   "On that, says he, perhaps sir you may not have been correctly informed."
I had received the information in Virginia from Colo
Harrison on his return from that Congress.   Lee,
Livingston & Jay had been the commee for that
draught.   The first, prepared by Lee, had been disapproved & recommitted.   The second was drawn
by Jay, but being presented by Govr Livingston,
had led Colo Harrison into the error.   The next
morning, walking in the hall of Congress, many members being assembled but the house not yet formed,
I observed Mr. Jay, speaking to R. H. Lee, and
leading him by the button of his coat, to me.   "I understand, sir, said he to me, that this gentleman informed you that Govr Livingston drew the Address
to the people of Gr Britain."   I assured him at once
that I had not received that information from Mr.
Lee & that not a word had ever passed on the subject
between Mr. Lee & myself; and after some explanations the subject was dropt.   These gentlemen had
had some sparrings in debate before, and continued
ever very hostile to each other.

I prepared a draught of the Declaration committed
to us.[1]   It was too strong for Mr. Dickinson.   He
still retained the hope of reconciliation with the

[1] *Cf.* note on Jefferson's draft, *post*, under July 6, 1775.

mother country, and was unwilling it should be lessened by offensive statements.   He was so honest a man, & so able a one that he was greatly indulged even by those who could not feel his scruples.   We therefore requested him to take the paper, and put it into a form he could approve.   He did so, preparing an entire new statement, and preserving of the former only the last 4. paragraphs & half of the preceding one.   We approved & reported it to Congress, who accepted it.   Congress gave a signal proof of their indulgence to Mr. Dickinson, and of their great desire not to go too fast for any respectable part of our body, in permitting him to draw their second petition to the king according to his own ideas,[1] and passing it with scarcely any amendment. The disgust against this humility was general; and Mr. Dickinson's delight at its passage was the only circumstance which reconciled them to it.   The vote being passed, altho' further observn on it was out of order, he could not refrain from rising and expressing his satisfaction and concluded by saying "there is but one word, Mr. President, in the paper which I disapprove, & that is the word *Congress*," on which Ben Harrison rose and said "there is but one word in the paper, Mr. President, of which I approve, and that is the word *Congress*."

On the 22d of July Dr. Franklin, Mr. Adams, R. H. Lee, & myself, were appointed a commee to consider and report on Ld. North's conciliatory resolution.   The answer of the Virginia assembly on that subject having been approved I was requested by

[1] "Scarcely I believe altering one" struck out in MS. by author.

the commee to prepare this report, which will account for the similarity of feature in the two instruments.[1]

On the 15th of May, 1776, the convention of Virginia instructed their delegates in Congress to propose to that body to declare the colonies independent of G. Britain, and appointed a commee to prepare a declaration of rights and plan of government.[2]

[3] In Congress, Friday June 7. 1776.   The delegates from Virginia moved [4] in obedience to instructions from their constituents that the Congress should declare that these United colonies are & of right ought to be free & independent states, that they are absolved from all allegiance to the British crown, and that all political connection between them & the state of Great Britain is & ought to be, totally dissolved; that measures should be immediately taken for procuring the assistance of foreign powers, and a Confederation be formed to bind the colonies more closely together.[5]

[1] See *post*, under July 31, 1775.

[2] Printed in Force's *Archives*, 5th, VI, 461.

[3] Here, in the original manuscript, commence the "two preceding sheets" referred to by Mr. Jefferson, as containing "notes" taken by him "whilst these things were going on." They are easily distinguished from the body of the MS. in which they were inserted by him, being of a paper very different in size, quality, and color from that on which the latter is written.

[4] Introduced by Richard Henry Lee. His autograph resolution is reproduced in Etting's *Memorials of 1776*, p. 4.

[5] "The Congress sat till 7 o'clock this evening in consequence of a motion of R. H. Lee's rendering ourselves free and independent States. The sensible part of the House opposed the Motion—they had no objection to forming a Scheme of a Treaty which they would send to France by proper Persons & uniting this Continent by a Confederacy; they saw no wisdom in a Declaration of Independence, nor any other

The house being obliged to attend at that time
to some other business, the proposition was referred
to the next day, when the members were ordered to
attend punctually at ten o'clock.

Saturday June 8.   They proceeded to take it into
consideration and referred it to a committee of the
whole, into which they immediately resolved themselves, and passed that day & Monday the 10th in
debating on the subject.

It was argued by Wilson, Robert R. Livingston,
E. Rutledge, Dickinson and others

That tho' they were friends to the measures themselves, and saw the impossibility that we should ever
again be united with Gr. Britain, yet they were
against adopting them at this time:

That the conduct we had formerly observed was
wise & proper now, of deferring to take any capital
step till the voice of the people drove us into it:

That they were our power, & without them our
declarations could not be carried into effect;

That the people of the middle colonies (Maryland,
Delaware, Pennsylva, the Jerseys & N. York) were

Purpose to be enforced by it, but placing ourselves in the power of
those with whom we mean to treat, giving our Enemy Notice of our
Intentions before we had taken any steps to execute them.   The event,
however, was that the Question was postponed; it is to be renewed on
Monday when I mean to move that it should be postponed for 3 Weeks
or Months.   In the mean Time the plan of Confederation & the Scheme
of Treaty may go on.   I don't know whether I shall succeed in this
Motion; I think not, it is at least doubtful.   However I must do what
is right in my own Eyes, & Consequences must take Care of themselves.
I wish you had been here—the whole Argument was sustained on one
side by R. Livingston, Wilson, Dickenson, & myself, & by the Power
of all N. England, Virginia & Georgia at the other."—*E. Rutledge to
John Jay, June 8, 1776.*

not yet ripe for bidding adieu to British connection, but that they were fast ripening & in a short time would join in the general voice of America:

That the resolution entered into by this house on the 15th of May [1] for suppressing the exercise of all powers derived from the crown, had shown, by the ferment into which it had thrown these middle colonies, that they had not yet accommodated their minds to a separation from the mother country:

That some of them had expressly forbidden their delegates to consent to such a declaration, and others had given no instructions, & consequently no powers to give such consent:

That if the delegates of any particular colony had no power to declare such colony independant, certain they were the others could not declare it for them; the colonies being as yet perfectly independant of each other:

That the assembly of Pennsylvania was now sitting above stairs, their convention would sit within a few days, the convention of New York was now sitting, & those of the Jerseys & Delaware counties would meet on the Monday following, & it was probable these bodies would take up the question of Independance & would declare to their delegates the voice of their state:

---

[1] That "every kind of authority under the said crown should be totally suppressed" and "to adopt such government as shall . . . best conduce to the happiness and safety of their constituents."— *Journal of Congress*, II., 166, 174. Duane, in a letter to Jay, dated May 16th, states that: "it has occasioned a great alarm here [Philadelphia], and the cautious folks are very fearful of its being attended with many ill consequences."

That if such a declaration should now be agreed to, these delegates must retire & possibly their colonies might secede from the Union:

That such a secession would weaken us more than could be compensated by any foreign alliance:

That in the event of such a division, foreign powers would either refuse to join themselves to our fortunes, or, having us so much in their power as that desperate declaration would place us, they would insist on terms proportionably more hard and prejudicial:

That we had little reason to expect an alliance with those to whom alone as yet we had cast our eyes:

That France & Spain had reason to be jealous of that rising power which would one day certainly strip them of all their American possessions:

That it was more likely they should form a connection with the British court, who, if they should find themselves unable otherwise to extricate themselves from their difficulties, would agree to a partition of our territories, restoring Canada to France, & the Floridas to Spain, to accomplish for themselves a recovery of these colonies:

That it would not be long before we should receive certain information of the disposition of the French court, from the agent whom we had sent to Paris for that purpose:

That if this disposition should be favorable, by waiting the event of the present campaign, which we all hoped would be successful, we should have reason to expect an alliance on better terms:

That this would in fact work no delay of any effectual aid from such ally, as, from the advance of the season & distance of our situation, it was impossible we could receive any assistance during this campaign:

That it was prudent to fix among ourselves the terms on which we should form alliance, before we declared we would form one at all events:

And that if these were agreed on, & our Declaration of Independance ready by the time our Ambassador should be prepared to sail, it would be as well as to go into that Declaration at this day.

On the other side it was urged by J. Adams, Lee, Wythe, and others

That no gentleman had argued against the policy or the right of separation from Britain, nor had supposed it possible we should ever renew our connection; that they had only opposed its being now declared:

That the question was not whether, by a declaration of independance, we should make ourselves what we are not; but whether we should declare a fact which already exists:

That as to the people or parliament of England, we had alwais been independent of them, their restraints on our trade deriving efficacy from our acquiescence only, & not from any rights they possessed of imposing them, & that so far our connection had been federal only & was now dissolved by the commencement of hostilities:

That as to the King, we had been bound to him by allegiance, but that this bond was now dissolved by his assent to the late act of parliament, by which he declares us out of his protection, and by his levying

war on us, a fact which had long ago proved us out
of his protection; it being a certain position in law
that allegiance & protection are reciprocal, the one
ceasing when the other is withdrawn:

That James the IId. never declared the people of
England out of his protection yet his actions proved
it & the parliament declared it:

No delegates then can be denied, or ever want, a
power of declaring an existing truth:

That the delegates from the Delaware counties
having declared their constituents ready to join, there
are only two colonies Pennsylvania & Maryland
whose delegates are absolutely tied up, and that
these had by their instructions only reserved a right
of confirming or rejecting the measure:

That the instructions from Pennsylvania might be
accounted for from the times in which they were
drawn, near a twelvemonth ago, since which the face
of affairs has totally changed:

That within that time it had become apparent that
Britain was determined to accept nothing less than
a carte-blanche, and that the King's answer to the
Lord Mayor Aldermen & common council of London,
which had come to hand four days ago, must have
satisfied every one of this point:

That the people wait for us to lead the way:

That *they* are in favour of the measure, tho' the instructions given by some of their *representatives* are
not:

That the voice of the representatives is not always
consonant with the voice of the people, and that this
is remarkably the case in these middle colonies:

That the effect of the resolution of the 15th of May has proved this, which, raising the murmurs of some in the colonies of Pennsylvania & Maryland, called forth the opposing voice of the freer part of the people, & proved them to be the majority, even in these colonies:

That the backwardness of these two colonies might be ascribed partly to the influence of proprietary power & connections, & partly to their having not yet been attacked by the enemy:

That these causes were not likely to be soon removed, as there seemed no probability that the enemy would make either of these the seat of this summer's war:

That it would be vain to wait either weeks or months for perfect unanimity, since it was impossible that all men should ever become of one sentiment on any question:

That the conduct of some colonies from the beginning of this contest, had given reason to suspect it was their settled policy to keep in the rear of the confederacy, that their particular prospect might be better, even in the worst event:

That therefore it was necessary for those colonies who had thrown themselves forward & hazarded all from the beginning, to come forward now also, and put all again to their own hazard:

That the history of the Dutch revolution, of whom three states only confederated at first proved that a secession of some colonies would not be so dangerous as some apprehended:

That a declaration of Independence alone could

render it consistent with European delicacy for European powers to treat with us, or even to receive an Ambassador from us:

That till this they would not receive our vessels into their ports, nor acknowledge the adjudications of our courts of admiralty to be legitimate, in cases of capture of British vessels:

That though France & Spain may be jealous of our rising power, they must think it will be much more formidable with the addition of Great Britain; and will therefore see it their interest to prevent a coalition; but should they refuse, we shall be but where we are; whereas without trying we shall never know whether they will aid us or not:

That the present campaign may be unsuccessful, & therefore we had better propose an alliance while our affairs wear a hopeful aspect:

That to await the event of this campaign will certainly work delay, because during this summer France may assist us effectually by cutting off those supplies of provisions from England & Ireland on which the enemy's armies here are to depend; or by setting in motion the great power they have collected in the West Indies, & calling our enemy to the defence of the possessions they have there:

That it would be idle to lose time in settling the terms of alliance, till we had first determined we would enter into alliance:

That it is necessary to lose no time in opening a trade for our people, who will want clothes, and will want money too for the paiment of taxes:

And that the only misfortune is that we did not

enter into alliance with France six months sooner, as besides opening their ports for the vent of our last year's produce, they might have marched an army into Germany and prevented the petty princes there from selling their unhappy subjects to subdue us.

It appearing in the course of these debates that the colonies of N. York, New Jersey, Pennsylvania, Delaware, Maryland, and South Carolina [1] were not yet matured for falling from the parent stem, but that they were fast advancing to that state, it was thought most prudent to wait a while for them, and to postpone the final decision to July 1. but that this might occasion as little delay as possible a committee was appointed [2] to prepare a declaration of independence. The commee were J. Adams, Dr. Franklin, Roger Sherman, Robert R. Livingston & myself. Committees were also appointed at the same time to prepare a plan of confederation for the colonies, and to state the terms proper to be proposed for foreign alliance. The committee for drawing the declaration of Independence desired me to do it. It was accordingly done, and being approved by them, I reported it to the house on Friday the 28th of June when it was read and ordered to lie on the table.[3] On

[1] "Had not yet advanced to" struck out in MS. by author.

[2] June 10, 1776.

[3] A different account is given of this by John Adams, as follows:

"The committee had several meetings, in which were proposed the articles of which the declaration was to consist, and minutes made of them. The committee then appointed Mr. Jefferson and me to draw them up in form, and clothe them in a proper dress. The sub-committee met, and considered the minutes, making such observations on them as then occurred, when Mr. Jefferson desired me to take them to my lodgings, and make the draught. This I declined, and gave several

Monday, the 1st of July the house resolved itself into a commee of the whole & resumed the consideration of the original motion made by the delegates of

reasons for declining. 1. That he was a Virginian, and I a Massachusettensian. 2. That he was a southern man, and I a northern one. 3. That I had been so obnoxious for my early and constant zeal in promoting the measure, that any draught of mine would undergo a more severe scrutiny and criticism in Congress, than one of his composition. 4. And lastly, and that would be reason enough if there were no other, I had a great opinion of the elegance of his pen, and none at all of my own. I therefore insisted that no hesitation should be made on his part. He accordingly took the minutes, and in a day or two produced to me his draught. Whether I made or suggested any correction, I remember not. The report was made to the committee of five, by them examined, but, whether altered or corrected in any thing, I cannot recollect. But, in substance at least, it was reported to Congress, where, after a severe criticism, and striking out several of the most oratorical paragraphs, it was adopted on the fourth of July, 1776, and published to the world."—*Autobiography of John Adams.*

"You inquire why so young a man as Mr. Jefferson was placed at the head of the Committee for preparing a Declaration of Independence? I answer: it was the Frankfort advice, to place Virginia at the head of every thing. Mr. Richard Henry Lee might be gone to Virgina, to his sick family, for aught I know, but that was not the reason of Mr. Jefferson's appointment. There were three committees appointed at the same time. One for the Declaration of Independence, another for preparing the articles of Confederation, another for preparing a treaty to be proposed to France. Mr. Lee was chosen for the committee of Confederation, and it was not thought convenient that the same person should be upon both. Mr. Jefferson came into Congress, in June, 1775, and brought with him a reputation for literature, science, and a happy talent of composition. Writings of his were handed about, remarkable for the peculiar felicity of expression. Though a silent member in Congress, he was so prompt, frank, explicit, and decisive upon committees and in conversation, not even Samuel Adams was more so, that he soon seized upon my heart and upon this occasion I gave him my vote, and did all in my power to procure the votes of others. I think he had one more vote than any other, and that placed him at the head of the committee. I had the next highest number, and that placed me the second. The committee met, discussed the subject, and then appointed Mr. Jefferson and me to make the draft, I suppose because we were the two first on the list.

"The sub-committee met. Jefferson proposed to me to make the

Virginia, which being again debated through the
day, was carried in the affirmative by the votes of
N. Hampshire, Connecticut, Massachusetts, Rhode
Island, N. Jersey, Maryland, Virginia, N. Carolina, &

draft. I said: 'I will not.' 'You should do it.' 'Oh! no.' 'Why
will you not? You ought to do it.' 'I will not.' 'Why?' 'Reasons
enough.' 'What can be your reasons?' 'Reason first—You are a
Virginian, and a Virginian ought to appear at the head of this business.
Reason second—I am obnoxious, suspected, and unpopular. You are
very much otherwise. Reason third—You can write ten times better
than I can.' 'Well,' said Jefferson, 'If you are decided, I will do as
well as I can.' 'Very well. When you have drawn it up, we will have
a meeting.'

"A meeting we accordingly had, and conned the paper over. I was
delighted with its high tone and the flights of oratory with which it
abounded, especially that concerning negro slavery, which, though I
knew his Southern brethren would never suffer to pass in Congress,
I certainly never would oppose. There were other expressions which I
would not have inserted, if I had drawn it up, particularly that which
called the King tyrant. I thought this too personal; for I never believed George to be a tyrant in disposition and in nature; I always believed him to be deceived by his courtiers on both sides of the Atlantic,
and in his official capacity only, cruel. I thought the expression too
passionate, and too much like scolding, for so grave and solemn a
document; but as Franklin and Sherman were to inspect it afterwards,
I thought it would not become me to strike it out. I consented to report it, and do not now remember that I made or suggested a single
alteration.

"We reported it to the committee of five. It was read, and I do not
remember that Franklin or Sherman criticised any thing. We were
all in haste. Congress was impatient, and the instrument was reported, as I believe, in Jefferson's handwriting, as he first drew it.
Congress cut off about a quarter of it, as I expected they would; but
they obliterated some of the best of it, and left all that was exception-
able, if anything in it was. I have long wondered that the original
draught has not been published. I suppose the reason is, the ve-
hement philippic against negro slavery."—*John Adams to Timothy
Pickering, Aug. 22, 1822.*

To this Jefferson replied:

"You have doubtless seen Timothy Pickering's fourth of July observations on the Declaration of Independence. If his principles and
prejudices, personal and political, gave us no reason to doubt whether

Georgia. S. Carolina and Pennsylvania voted against
it. Delaware having but two members present, they
were divided.[1] The delegates for New York de-

he had truly quoted the information he alleges to have received from
Mr. Adams, I should then say, that in some of the particulars, Mr.
Adams' memory has led him into unquestionable error. At the age
of eighty-eight, and forty-seven years after the transactions of Independence, this is not wonderful. Nor should I, at the age of eighty, on
the small advantage of that difference only, venture to oppose my
memory to his, were it not supported by written notes, taken by myself at the moment and on the spot. He says 'the committee of five,
to wit, Doctor Franklin, Sherman, Livingston and ourselves, met, discussed the subject, and then appointed him and myself to make the
draught; that we, as a sub-committee, met, and after the urgencies
of each on the other, I consented to undertake the task, that the
draught being made, we, the sub-committee, met, and conned the
paper over, and he does not remember that he made or suggested a
single alteration.' Now these details are quite incorrect. The committee of five met; no such thing as a sub-committee was proposed, but
they unanimously pressed on myself alone to undertake the draught.
I consented; I drew it; but before I reported it to the committee, I
communicated it *separately* to Doctor Franklin and Mr. Adams, requesting their corrections because they were the two members of
whose judgments and amendments I wished most to have the benefit,
before presenting it to the committee: and you have seen the original
paper now in my hands, with the corrections of Doctor Franklin and
Mr. Adams interlined in their own handwritings. Their alterations
were two or three only, and merely verbal. I then wrote a fair copy,
reported it to the committee, and from them unaltered, to Congress.
This personal communication and consultation with Mr. Adams, he
has misremembered into the actings of a sub-committee. Pickering's
observations, and Mr. Adams' in addition, 'that it contained no new
ideas, that it is a common place compilation, its sentiments hacknied
in Congress for two years before, and its essence contained in Otis'
pamphlet,' may all be true. Of that I am not to be the judge. Richard Henry Lee charged it as copied from Locke's treatise on government. Otis' pamphlet I never saw, and whether I had gathered my
ideas from reading or reflection I do not know. I know only that I
turned to neither book nor pamphlet while writing it. I did not consider it as any part of my charge to invent new ideas altogether, and
to offer no sentiment which had ever been expressed before."—*Letter
to J. Madison, Aug. 30, 1823.*

[1] George Read (opposing) and Thomas McKean.

clared they were for it themselves & were assured
their constituents were for it, but that their instructions having been drawn near a twelvemonth before,
when reconciliation was still the general object, they
were enjoined by them to do nothing which should
impede that object.   They therefore thought themselves not justifiable in voting on either side, and
asked leave to withdraw from the question, which
was given them.   The commee rose & reported their
resolution to the house.   Mr. Edward Rutledge of S.
Carolina then requested the determination might be
put off to the next day, as he believed his colleagues,
tho' they disapproved of the resolution, would then
join in it for the sake of unanimity.   The ultimate
question whether the house would agree to the resolution of the committee was accordingly postponed
to the next day, when it was again moved and S. Carolina concurred in voting for it.   In the meantime a
third member had come post from the Delaware counties [1] and turned the vote of that colony in favour of
the resolution.   Members [2] of a different sentiment
attending that morning from Pennsylvania also, their
vote was changed, so that the whole 12 colonies who
were authorized to vote at all, gave their voices for it;
and within a few days,[3] the convention of N. York
approved of it and thus supplied the void occasioned
by the withdrawing of her delegates from the vote.

Congress proceeded the same day [4] to consider the

[1] Cæsar Rodney.
[2] Dickinson and Robert Morris did not attend, Wilson changed his
vote, and with Franklin and Morton, outvoted Willing and Humphreys.
[3] July 9th.
[4] Monday, July 1st.   No sitting was held on Saturday.

declaration of Independance which had been reported & lain on the table the Friday preceding, and on Monday referred to a commee of the whole. The pusillanimous idea that we had friends in England worth keeping terms with, still haunted the minds of many. For this reason those passages which conveyed censures on the people of England were struck out, lest they should give them offence. The clause too, reprobating the enslaving the inhabitants of Africa, was struck out in complaisance to South Carolina and Georgia, who had never attempted to restrain the importation of slaves, and who on the contrary still wished to continue it. Our northern brethren also I believe felt a little tender under those censures; for tho' their people have very few slaves themselves yet they had been pretty considerable carriers of them to others. The debates having taken up the greater parts of the 2d 3d & 4th days of July were,[1] in the evening of the last, closed the declaration was reported by the commee, agreed to by the house and signed by every member present except Mr. Dickinson.[2] As the sentiments of men are known not only by what they receive, but what they

[1] The "Resolution" for independence was under discussion on the 1st of July. The declaration on July 2d, 3d, and 4th.

[2] The question whether the declaration was signed on the 4th of July, as well as on the 2d of August, has been a much vexed one, but a careful study of it must make almost certain that it was not. The MS. *Journal of Congress* (that printed by order of Congress being fabricated and altered) merely required its "authentication," which we know from other cases was by the signatures of the president and secretary; who accordingly signed it "by order and in behalf of the Congress," and the printed copies at once sent out had only these signatures. It is also certain that several of the members then in Con-

reject also, I will state the form of the declaration as
originally reported. The parts struck out by Congress shall be distinguished by a black line drawn
under them; & those inserted by them shall be placed
in the margin or in a concurrent column.[1]

gress would have refused to sign it on that day, and that the Congress
therefore had good cause to postpone the signing till certain of the
delegations should receive new instructions, or be changed; and also
till its first effect on the people might be seen. For these reasons the
declaration was not even entered in the journal, though a blank was
left for it, and when it was inserted at a later period, the list of signers
was taken from the engrossed copy, though had there been one signed
on the 4th of July it would certainly have been the one printed from,
as including the men who were in Congress on that day and who voted
on the question, instead of one signed by a number of men who were
neither present nor members when the declaration was adopted.
Moreover, though the printed journal afterwards led John Adams to
believe and state that the declaration was signed on the 4th, we have
his contemporary statement, on July 9th, that "as soon as an American seal is prepared, I conjecture the Declaration will be subscribed
by all the members." And we have the positive denial of McKean
that "no person signed it on that day," and this statement is substan-
tiated by the later action of Congress in specially permitting him to
sign what he certainly would have already done on the 4th, had there
been the opportunity. Opposed to these direct statements and prob-
abilities, we have Jefferson's positive statement, three times repeated,
that such a signing took place, but as he follows his nearly contemporary one with the statements that it was "signed by every member
present except Mr. Dickinson," when we have proof positive that all
the New York delegates refused to even vote, much less sign, and that
Dickinson was not even present in Congress on that day, it is evident
that this narrative is not wholly trustworthy.

[1] "I expected you had in the Preamble to our form of Government,
exhausted the subject of complaint agt Geo. 3d & was at a loss to
discover what Congress would do for one to their Declaration of Independence without copying, but find you have acquitted your selves
very well on that score."—E. Pendleton to Jefferson, July 22.
"I am also obliged by ye Original Declaration of Independence,
which I find your brethren have treated as they did ye Manifesto last
summer—altered it much for the worse; their hopes of a Reconciliation
might restrain them from plain truths then, but what could cramp
them now?"—E. Pendleton to Jefferson, Aug. 10, 1776.

A DECLARATION BY THE REPRESENTATIVES OF THE
UNITED STATES OF AMERICA, IN GENERAL
CONGRESS ASSEMBLED

When in the course of human events it becomes
necessary for one people to dissolve the political
bands which have connected them with another,
and to assume among the powers of the earth the
separate & equal station to which the laws of nature and of nature's God entitle them, a decent respect to the opinions of mankind requires that they
should declare the causes which impel them to the
separation.

We hold these truths to be self-evident: that all
men are created equal; that they are endowed by
their creator with inherent and inalienable   certain
rights; that among these are life, liberty,
& the pursuit of happiness: that to secure these
rights, governments are instituted among men, deriving their just powers from the consent of the
governed; that whenever any form of government
becomes destructive of these ends, it is the right of
the people to alter or abolish it, & to institute new
government, laying it's foundation on such principles, & organizing it's powers in such form, as to
them shall seem most likely to effect their safety &
happiness. Prudence indeed will dictate that governments long established should not be changed for
light & transient causes; and accordingly all experience hath shown that mankind are more disposed
to suffer while evils are sufferable, than to right themselves by abolishing the forms to which they are

accustomed. But when a long train of abuses &
usurpations begun at a distinguished period and
pursuing invariably the same object, evinces a design to reduce them under absolute despotism, it is
their right, it is their duty to throw off such government, & to provide new guards for their future security. Such has been the patient sufferance of these
colonies; & such is now the necessity which con-
_{alter} strains them to expunge their former
systems of government. The history of the
present king of Great Britain is a history of un-
_{repeated} remitting injuries & usurpations, among
which appears no solitary fact to contradict the
_{all having} uniform tenor of the rest but all have in
direct object the establishment of an absolute
tyranny over these states. To prove this let facts
be submitted to a candid world for the truth of which
we pledge a faith yet unsullied by falsehood.

He has refused his assent to laws the most wholesome & necessary for the public good.

He has forbidden his governors to pass laws of
immediate & pressing importance, unless suspended
in their operation till his assent should be obtained;
& when so suspended, he has utterly neglected to
attend to them.

He has refused to pass other laws for the accommodation of large districts of people, unless those
people would relinquish the right of representation
in the legislature, a right inestimable to them, &
formidable to tyrants only.

He has called together legislative bodies at places
unusual, uncomfortable, and distant from the deposi-

tory of their public records, for the sole purpose of fatiguing them into compliance with his measures.

He has dissolved representative houses repeatedly & continually for opposing with manly firmness his invasions on the rights of the people.

He has refused for a long time after such dissolutions to cause others to be elected, whereby the legislative powers, incapable of annihilation, have returned to the people at large for their exercise, the state remaining in the meantime exposed to all the dangers of invasion from without & convulsions within.

He has endeavored to prevent the population of these states; for that purpose obstructing the laws for naturalization of foreigners, refusing to pass others to encourage their migrations hither, & raising the conditions of new appropriations of lands.

He has suffered the administration of   obstructed
justice totally to cease in some of these   by
states refusing his assent to laws for establishing judiciary powers.

He has made our judges dependant on his will alone, for the tenure of their offices, & the amount & paiment of their salaries.

He has erected a multitude of new offices by a self assumed power and sent hither swarms of new officers to harass our people and eat out their substance.

He has kept among us in times of peace standing armies and ships of war without the consent of our legislatures.

He has affected to render the military independant of, & superior to the civil power.

He has combined with others to subject us to a jurisdiction foreign to our constitutions & unacknowledged by our laws, giving his assent to their acts of pretended legislation for quartering large bodies of armed troops among us; for protecting them by a mock-trial from punishment for any murders which they should commit on the inhabitants of these states; for cutting off our trade with all parts of the world; for imposing taxes on us without _{in many cases} our consent; for depriving us [ ] of the benefits of trial by jury; for transporting us beyond seas to be tried for pretended offences; for abolishing the free system of English laws in a neighboring province, establishing therein an arbitrary government, and enlarging it's boundaries, so as to render it at once an example and fit instrument for introducing the same absolute _{colonies} rule into these states; for taking away our charters, abolishing our most valuable laws, and altering fundamentally the forms of our governments; for suspending our own legislatures, & declaring themselves invested with power to legislate for us in all cases whatsoever.

_{by declaring us out of his protection, and waging war against us.} He has abdicated government here withdrawing his governors, and declaring us out of his allegiance & protection.

He has plundered our seas, ravaged our coasts, burnt our towns, & destroyed the lives of our people.

He is at this time transporting large armies of foreign mercenaries to compleat the works of death, desolation & tyranny already begun with circum-

stances of cruelty and perfidy [ ] unworthy the head
of a civilized nation.   scarcely
                                              paralleled in
He has constrained our fellow citizens   the most
                                              barbarous
taken captive on the high seas to bear arms   ages, &
                                              totally
against their country, to become the executioners of
their friends & brethren, or to fall themselves by
their hands.

He has [ ] endeavored to bring on the   excited
inhabitants of our frontiers the merciless   domestic in-
                                             surrection
                                             among us,
Indian savages, whose known rule of war-   & has
fare is an undistinguished destruction of all ages,
sexes, & conditions of existence.

He has incited treasonable insurrections of our
fellow-citizens, with the allurements of forfeiture &
confiscation of our property.

He has waged cruel war against human nature
itself, violating it's most sacred rights of life and
liberty in the persons of a distant people who never
offended him, captivating & carrying them into
slavery in another hemisphere, or to incur miserable
death in their transportation thither.   This piratical
warfare, the opprobium of INFIDEL powers, is the
warfare of the CHRISTIAN king of Great Britain.   Determined to keep open a market where MEN should
be bought & sold, he has prostituted his negative for
suppressing every legislative attempt to prohibit or
to restrain this execrable commerce.   And that this
assemblage of horrors might want no fact of distinguished die, he is now exciting those very people to
rise in arms among us, and to purchase that liberty
of which he has deprived them, by murdering the
people on whom he also obtruded them: thus paying

off former crimes committed against the LIBERTIES of one people, with crimes which he urges them to commit against the LIVES of another.

In every stage of these oppressions we have petitioned for redress in the most humble terms: our repeated petitions have been answered only by repeated injuries.

A prince whose character is thus marked by every act which may define a tyrant is unfit to be the ruler ^{free} of a [ ] people who mean to be free. Future ages will scarcely believe that the hardiness of one man adventured, within the short compass of twelve years only, to lay a foundation so broad & so undisguised for tyranny over a people fostered & fixed in principles of freedom.

Nor have we been wanting in attention to our British brethren. We have warned them from time ^{an unwar-rantable} to time of attempts by their legislature to ^{us} extend a jurisdiction over these our states. We have reminded them of the circumstances of our emigration & settlement here, no one of which could warrant so strange a pretension: that these were effected at the expense of our own blood & treasure, unassisted by the wealth or the strength of Great Britain: that in constituting indeed our several forms of government, we had adopted one common king, thereby laying a foundation for perpetual league & amity with them: but that submission to their parliament was no part of our constitution, nor ever in ^{have} idea, if history may be credited: and, we [ ] ^{and we have conjured them by} appealed to their native justice and magnanimity as well as to the ties of our common

kindred to disavow these usurpations which were
likely to interrupt our connection and cor- would in-
respondence.   They too have been deaf to evitably
the voice of justice & of consanguinity, and when
occasions have been given them, by the regular
course of their laws, of removing from their councils the disturbers of our harmony, they have, by
their free election, re-established them in power.
At this very time too they are permitting their
chief magistrate to send over not only soldiers of
our common blood, but Scotch & foreign mercenaries to invade & destroy us.   These facts have given
the last stab to agonizing affection, and manly spirit
bids us to renounce forever these unfeeling brethren.
We must endeavor to forget our former love for them,
and hold them as we hold the rest of mankind, enemies in war, in peace friends.   We might have been
a free and a great people together; but a communication of grandeur & of freedom it seems is below
their dignity.   Be it so, since they will have it.   The
road to happiness & to glory is open to us too.   We
will tread it apart from them, and ac- We must therefore
quiesce in the necessity which de- and hold them as
we hold the rest of
nuonces our eternal separation [ ] ! mankind, enemies
in war, in peace
friends.

We therefore the repre-	We therefore the repre-
sentatives of the United	sentatives of the United
States of America in Gen-	States of America in Gen-
eral Congress assembled	eral Congress assembled,
do in the name & by au-	appealing to the supreme
thority of the good people	judge of the world for the
of these states reject &	rectitude of our inten-

renounce all allegiance & subjection to the kings of Great Britain & all others who may hereafter claim by, through or under them: we utterly dissolve all political connection which may heretofore have subsisted between us & the people or parliament of Great Britain: & finally we do assert & declare these colonies to be free & independent states, & that as free & independent states, they have full power to levy war, conclude peace, contract alliances, establish commerce, & to do all other acts & things which independent states may of right do.

And for the support of this declaration we mutually pledge to each other our lives, our fortunes, & our sacred honor.

tions, do in the name, & by the authority of the good people of these colonies, solemnly publish & declare that these united colonies are & of right ought to be free & independent states; that they are absolved from all allegiance to the British crown, and that all political connection between them & the state of Great Britain is, & ought to be, totally dissolved; & that as free & independent states they have full power to levy war, conclude peace, contract alliances, establish commerce & to do all other acts & things which independant states may of right do.

And for the support of this declaration, with a firm reliance on the protection of divine providence we mutually pledge to each other our lives, our fortunes, & our sacred honor.[1]

---

[1] This is printed just as Jefferson prepared it for the press. By

The Declaration thus signed on the 4th, on paper was engrossed on parchment, & signed again on the 2d. of August.[1]

On Friday July 12. the Committee appointed to draw the articles of confederation reported them, and on the 22d. the house resolved themselves into a committee to take them into consideration. On the 30th. & 31st. of that month & 1st. of the ensuing, those articles were debated which determined the proportion or quota of money which each state should furnish to the common treasury, and the manner of voting in Congress. The first of these articles was expressed in the original draught in these words.[2] "Art. XI. All charges of war & all

comparing it with the text as printed *post*, under July 4, 1776, it will be seen that he took the liberty of somewhat changing and even expunging portions.

[1] This is an interlineation made at a later period—apparently after the question as to the signing of the declaration was raised. Jefferson has also written the following on a slip and pasted it on the sheet:

"Some erroneous statements of the proceedings on the declaration of independence having got before the public in latter times, Mr. Samuel A. Wells asked explanations of me, which are given in my letter to him of May 12. 19. before and now again referred to. I took notes in my place while these things were going on, and at their close wrote them out in form and with correctness and from 1 to 7 of the two preceding sheets are the originals then written; as the two following are of the earlier debates on the Confederation, which I took in like manner."

[2] In the *Works of John Adams* (ii., 492) are printed his memoranda of the debates on the confederation, wherein he has recorded the following sentences from Jefferson's speeches on that subject: Article 14. "The limits of the Southern Colonies are fixed. Moves an amendment, that all purchases of lands, not within the boundaries of any Colony, shall be made by Congress of the Indians in a great Council." Article 15. "What are reasonable limits? What security have we, that the Congress will not curtail the present settlements of the States?

other expenses that shall be incurred for the common
defence, or general welfare, and allowed by the
United States assembled, shall be defrayed out of
a common treasury, which shall be supplied by the
several colonies in proportion to the number of inhabitants of every age, sex & quality, except Indians
not paying taxes, in each colony, a true account of
which, distinguishing the white inhabitants, shall be
triennially taken & transmitted to the Assembly
of the United States."

Mr. [Samuel] Chase moved that the quotas should
be fixed, not by the number of inhabitants of every
condition, but by that of the "white inhabitants."
He admitted that taxation should be alwais in proportion to property, that this was in theory the true
rule, but that from a variety of difficulties, it was a
rule which could never be adopted in practice. The
value of the property in every State could never be
estimated justly & equally. Some other measure
for the wealth of the State must therefore be devised,
some standard referred to which would be more simple. He considered the number of inhabitants as a
tolerably good criterion of property, and that this
might alwais be obtained. He therefore thought it
the best mode which we could adopt, with one exception only. He observed that negroes are prop-

I have no doubt that the colonies will limit themselves." Article 16.
"Thinks the Congress will have a short meeting in the Fall and another
in the Spring." Article 17. "Explains it to mean the Indians who live
in the Colony. These are subject to the laws in some degree. . . .
I protest against the right of Congress to decide upon the right of Virginia. Virginia has released all claims to lands settled by Maryland,
&c."

erty, and as such cannot be distinguished from the lands or personalities held in those States where there are few slaves, that the surplus of profit which a Northern farmer is able to lay by, he invests in cattle, horses, &c. whereas a Southern farmer lays out that same surplus in slaves. There is no more reason therefore for taxing the Southern states on the farmer's head, & on his slave's head, than the Northern ones on their farmer's heads & the heads of their cattle, that the method proposed would therefore tax the Southern states according to their numbers & their wealth conjunctly, while the Northern would be taxed on numbers only: that negroes in fact should not be considered as members of the state more than cattle & that they have no more interest in it.

Mr. John Adams observed that the numbers of people were taken by this article as an index of the wealth of the state, & not as subjects of taxation, that as to this matter it was of no consequence by what name you called your people, whether by that of freemen or of slaves. That in some countries the labouring poor were called freemen, in others they were called slaves; but that the difference as to the state was imaginary only. What matters it whether a landlord employing ten labourers in his farm, gives them annually as much money as will buy them the necessaries of life, or gives them those necessaries at short hand. The ten labourers add as much wealth annually to the state increase it's exports as much in the one case as the other. Certainly 500 freemen produce no more profits, no greater surplus for the paiment of taxes than 500 slaves. Therefore the state in which are the labourers called freemen should be taxed no more than that in which are those called slaves. Suppose by any extraordinary operation of nature or of law one half the labourers of a state could in the course of one night be transformed into slaves: would the state be made the poorer or the less able to pay taxes? That the condition of the laboring poor in most countries, that of the fishermen particularly of the Northern states, is as abject as that of slaves. It is the number of labourers which produce the surplus for taxation, and numbers therefore indiscriminately, are the fair index of wealth. That it is the use of the word "property" here, & it's application to some of the people of the state, which produces the fallacy. How does the Southern farmer procure slaves? Either by importation or by purchase from his neighbor. If he imports a slave, he adds one to the number of labourers in his country, and proportionably to it's profits & abilities to pay taxes. If he buys from his neighbor it is only a transfer of a labourer from one farm to another, which does not change the annual produce of the state, & therefore should not change it's tax. That if a Northern farmer works ten labourers on his farm, he can, it is true, invest the surplus of ten men's labour in cattle: but so may the Southern farmer working ten slaves. That a state of one hundred thousand freemen can maintain no more cattle than one of one hundred thousand slaves. Therefore they have no more of that kind of property. That a slave may indeed from the custom of speech be more properly called the wealth of his master, than the free labourer might be called the wealth of his employer: but as to the state, both were equally it's wealth, and should therefore equally add to the quota of it's tax.

Mr. [Benjamin] Harrison proposed as a compromise, that two slaves should be counted as one freeman. He affirmed that slaves did not do so much work as freemen, and doubted if two effected more than one. That this was proved by the price of labor. The hire of a labourer in the Southern colonies being from 8 to £12. while in the Northern it was generally £24.

Mr. [James] Wilson said that if this amendment should take place the Southern colonies would have all the benefit of slaves, whilst the Northern ones would bear the burthen. That slaves increase the profits of a state, which the Southern states mean to take to themselves; that they also increase the burthen of defence, which would of course fall so much the heavier on the Northern. That slaves occupy the places of freemen and eat their food. Dismiss your slaves & freemen will take their places. It is our duty to lay every discouragement on the importation of slaves; but this amendment would give the jus trium liberorum to him who would import slaves. That other kinds of property were pretty equally distributed thro' all the colonies: there were as many cattle, horses, & sheep, in the North as the South, & South as the North; but not so as to slaves. That experience has shown that those colonies have been alwais able to pay most which have the most inhabitants, whether they be

black or white, and the practice of the Southern
colonies has alwais been to make every farmer pay
poll taxes upon all his labourers whether they be
black or white. He acknowledges indeed that freemen work the most; but they consume the most
also. They do not produce a greater surplus for
taxation. The slave is neither fed nor clothed so
expensively as a freeman. Again white women are
exempted from labor generally, but negro women
are not. In this then the Southern states have an
advantage as the article now stands. It has sometimes been said that slavery is necessary because the
commodities they raise would be too dear for market
if cultivated by freemen; but now it is said that the
labor of the slave is the dearest.

Mr. Payne ¹ urged the original resolution of Congress, to proportion the quotas of the states to the
number of souls.

Dr. [John] Witherspoon was of opinion that the
value of lands & houses was the best estimate of the
wealth of a nation, and that it was practicable to
obtain such a valuation. This is the true barometer
of wealth. The one now proposed is imperfect in itself,
and unequal between the States. It has been objected
that negroes eat the food of freemen & therefore
should be taxed. Horses also eat the food of freemen;
therefore they also should be taxed. It has been said
too that in carrying slaves into the estimate of the
taxes the state is to pay, we do no more than those
states themselves do, who alwais take slaves into the
estimate of the taxes the individual is to pay. But

¹ Robert Treat Paine.

the cases are not parallel. In the Southern colonies slaves pervade the whole colony; but they do not pervade the whole continent. That as to the original resolution of Congress to proportion the quotas according to the souls, it was temporary only, & related to the monies heretofore emitted: whereas we are now entering into a new compact, and therefore stand on original ground.

Aug. 1. The question being put the amendment proposed was rejected by the votes of N. Hampshire, Massachusetts, Rhode island, Connecticut, N. York, N. Jersey, & Pennsylvania, against those of Delaware, Maryland, Virginia, North & South Carolina. Georgia was divided.

The other article was in these words. "Art. XVII. In determining questions each colony shall have one vote."

July 30. 31. Aug. 1. Present 41. members. Mr. Chase observed that this article was the most likely to divide us of any one proposed in the draught then under consideration. That the larger colonies had threatened they would not confederate at all if their weight in congress should not be equal to the numbers of people they added to the confederacy; while the smaller ones declared against a union if they did not retain an equal vote for the protection of their rights. That it was of the utmost consequence to bring the parties together, as should we sever from each other, either no foreign power will ally with us at all, or the different states will form different alliances, and thus increase the horrors of those scenes of civil war and bloodshed which in such a state of separation & independance would render us a miserable people. That our importance, our interests, our peace required that we should confederate, and that mutual sacrifices should be made to effect a compromise of this difficult question. He was of opinion the smaller colonies would lose their rights, if they were not in some instances allowed an equal vote; and therefore that a discrimination should take place among the questions which would come before Congress.[1] That the smaller states should be secured in all questions concerning life or liberty & the greater ones in all respecting property. He therefore proposed that in votes relating to money, the voice of each colony should be proportioned to the number of its inhabitants.

Dr. Franklin [2] thought that the votes should be so proportioned in all cases. He took notice that the Delaware counties had bound up their Delegates to disagree to this article. He thought it a very extraordinary language to be held by any state, that they would not confederate with us unless we would let them dispose of our money. Certainly if we vote equally we ought to pay equally; but the smaller states will hardly purchase the privilege at this price. That had he lived in a state where the representation, originally equal, had become unequal by time & accident he might have submitted rather than disturb government; but that we should be very wrong to set out in this practice when it is in our power to establish what is right. That at the time of the

---

[1] "He therefore proposed" struck out in MS. by author.
[2] "Seconded the proposition" struck out in MS. by author.

Union between England and Scotland the latter had
made the objection which the smaller states now do.
But experience had proved that no unfairness had
ever been shown them. That their advocates had
prognosticated that it would again happen as in
times of old, that the whale would swallow Jonas,
but he thought the prediction reversed in event and
that Jonas had swallowed the whale, for the Scotch
had in fact got possession of the government and
gave laws to the English. He reprobated the original agreement of Congress to vote by colonies and
therefore was for their voting in all cases according
to the number of taxables.[1]

Dr. Witherspoon opposed every alteration of the
article. All men admit that a confederacy is
necessary. Should the idea get abroad that there
is likely to be no union among us, it will damp the
minds of the people, diminish the glory of our struggle, & lessen it's importance; because it will open to
our view future prospects of war & dissension among
ourselves. If an equal vote be refused, the smaller
states will become vassals to the larger; & all experience has shown that the vassals & subjects of
free states are the most enslaved. He instanced the
Helots of Sparta & the provinces of Rome. He observed that foreign powers discovering this blemish
would make it a handle for disengaging the smaller
states from so unequal a confederacy. That the
colonies should in fact be considered as individuals;
and that as such, in all disputes they should have an

---

[1] "So far going beyond Mr. Chase's proposition," struck out in MS.
by author.

equal vote; that they are now collected as individuals making a bargain with each other, & of course had a right to vote as individuals. That in the East India company they voted by persons, & not by their proportion of stock. That the Belgic confederacy voted by provinces. That in questions of war the smaller states were as much interested as the larger, & therefore should vote equally; and indeed that the larger states were more likely to bring war on the confederacy in proportion as their frontier was more extensive. He admitted that equality of representation was an excellent principle, but then it must be of things which are co-ordinate; that is, of things similar & of the same nature: that nothing relating to individuals could ever come before Congress; nothing but what would respect colonies. He distinguished between an incorporating & a federal union. The union of England was an incorporating one; yet Scotland had suffered by that union: for that it's inhabitants were drawn from it by the hopes of places & employments. Nor was it an instance of equality of representation; because while Scotland was allowed nearly a thirteenth of representation they were to pay only one fortieth of the land tax. He expressed his hopes that in the present enlightened state of men's minds we might expect a lasting confederacy, if it was founded on fair principles.

John Adams advocated the voting in proportion to numbers. He said that we stand here as the representatives of the people. That in some states the people are many, in others they are few; that

therefore their vote here should be proportioned to
the numbers from whom it comes. Reason, justice,
& equity never had weight enough on the face of the
earth to govern the councils of men. It is interest
alone which does it, and it is interest alone which can
be trusted. That therefore the interests within
doors should be the mathematical representatives of
the interests without doors. That the individuality
of the colonies is a mere sound. Does the individuality of a colony increase it's wealth or numbers. If it
does, pay equally. If it does not add weight in the
scale of the confederacy, it cannot add to their rights,
nor weigh in argument. A. has £50. B. £500. C.
£1000. in partnership. Is it just they should equally
dispose of the monies of the partnership? It has
been said we are independent individuals making a
bargain together. The question is not what we are
now, but what we ought to be when our bargain
shall be made. The confederacy is to make us one
individual only; it is to form us, like separate parcels
of metal, into one common mass. We shall no
longer retain our separate individuality, but become
a single individual as to all questions submitted to
the confederacy. Therefore all those reasons which
prove the justice & expediency of equal representation in other assemblies, hold good here. It has
been objected that a proportional vote will endanger
the smaller states. We answer that an equal vote
will endanger the larger. Virginia, Pennsylvania, &
Massachusetts are the three greater colonies. Consider their distance, their difference of produce,
of interests & of manners, & it is apparent they can

never have an interest or inclination to combine for
the oppression of the smaller.   That the smaller will
naturally divide on all questions with the larger.
Rhode isld, from it's relation, similarity & intercourse will generally pursue the same objects with
Massachusetts; Jersey, Delaware & Maryland, with
Pennsylvania.

Dr. [Benjamin] Rush took notice that the decay
of the liberties of the Dutch republic proceeded from
three causes.   1. The perfect unanimity requisite on
all occasions.   2. Their obligation to consult their
constituents.   3. Their voting by provinces.   This
last destroyed the equality of representation, and
the liberties of great Britain also are sinking from the
same defect.   That a part of our rights is deposited
in the hands of our legislatures.   There it was admitted there should be an equality of representation.
Another part of our rights is deposited in the hands
of Congress: why is it not equally necessary there
should be an equal representation there?   Were it
possible to collect the whole body of the people together, they would determine the questions submitted to them by their majority.   Why should not
the same majority decide when voting here by their
representatives?   The larger colonies are so provi-
dentially divided in situation as to render every fear
of their combining visionary.   Their interests are
different, & their circumstances dissimilar.   It is
more probable they will become rivals & leave it in
the power of the smaller states to give preponderance
to any scale they please.   The voting by the number
of free inhabitants will have one excellent effect, that

of inducing the colonies to discourage slavery & to encourage the increase of their free inhabitants.

Mr. [Stephen] Hopkins observed there were 4 larger, 4 smaller, & 4 middle-sized colonies. That the 4 largest would contain more than half the inhabitants of the confederated states, & therefore would govern the others as they should please. That history affords no instance of such a thing as equal representation. The Germanic body votes by states. The Helvetic body does the same; & so does the Belgic confederacy. That too little is known of the ancient confederations to say what was their practice.

Mr. Wilson thought that taxation should be in proportion to wealth, but that representation should accord with the number of freemen. That government is a collection or result of the wills of all. That if any government could speak the will of all, it would be perfect; and that so far as it departs from this it becomes imperfect. It has been said that Congress is a representation of states; not of individuals. I say that the objects of its care are all the individuals of the states. It is strange that annexing the name of "State" to ten thousand men, should give them an equal right with forty thousand. This must be the effect of magic, not of reason. As to those matters which are referred to Congress, we are not so many states, we are one large state. We lay aside our individuality, whenever we come here. The Germanic body is a burlesque on government; and their practice on any point is a sufficient authority & proof that it is wrong. The greatest imperfection in the constitution of the Belgic confederacy is their voting by provinces. The interest of the whole is constantly sacrificed to that of the small states. The history of the war in the reign of Q. Anne sufficiently proves this. It is asked shall nine colonies put it into the power of four to govern them as they please? I invert the question, and ask shall two millions of people put it in the power of one million to govern them as they please? It is pretended too that the smaller colonies will be in danger from the greater. Speak in honest language & say the minority will be in danger from the majority. And is there an assembly on earth where this danger may not be equally pretended? The truth is that our proceedings will then be consentaneous with the interests of the majority, and so they ought to be. The probability is much greater that the larger states will disagree than that they will combine. I defy the wit of man to invent a possible case or to suggest any one thing on earth which shall be for the interests of Virginia, Pennsylvania & Massachusetts, and which will not also be for the interest of the other states.[1]

These articles reported July 12. 76 were debated

[1] Here end the notes which Jefferson states were taken "while these things were going on, and at their close" were "written out in form and with correctness." Much of their value depends on the date of their writing, but there is nothing to show this, except negative evidence. The sheets were all written at the same time, which makes the writing after Aug. 1, 1776; while the misstatements as to the signing, and as to Dickinson's presence, would seem almost impossible unless greater time even than this had elapsed between the occurrence and the notes. The MS. is, moreover, considerably corrected and interlined, which would hardly be the case if merely a transcript of rough notes.

from day to day, & time to time for two years, were
ratified July 9, '78, by 10 states, by N. Jersey on the
26th. of Nov. of the same year, and by Delaware on
the 23d. of Feb. following. Maryland alone held off
2 years more, acceding to them Mar 1, 81. and thus
closing the obligation.

Our delegation had been renewed for the ensuing
year commencing Aug. 11. but the new government
was now organized, a meeting of the legislature was
to be held in Oct. and I had been elected a member
by my county. I knew that our legislation under
the regal government had many very vicious points
which urgently required reformation, and I thought
I could be of more use in forwarding that work. I
therefore retired from my seat in Congress on the 2d.
of Sep. resigned it, and took my place in the legislature of my state, on the 7th. of October.

On the 11th.[1] I moved for leave to bring in a bill
for the establishment of courts of justice, the organization of which was of importance; I drew the
bill it was approved by the commee, reported and
passed after going thro' it's due course.[2]

[1] *Ordered*, That leave be given to bring in a bill *For the establishment
of courts of justice* within this Commonwealth, and that Mr. *Jefferson*,
Mr. *Smith*, Mr. *Bullitt*, Mr. *Fleming*, Mr. *Watts*, Mr. *Williams*, Mr. *Gray*,
Mr. *Bland*, Mr. *Braxton*, and Mr. *Curle* do prepare and bring in the
same.—*Journal of the House of Delegates, 1776*, p. 12.

[2] This is erroneously stated. After the committee was formed they
were directed by the House of Delegates to "divide the subject thereof
into five distinct bills." Three of these. ("Appeals," "Chancery," and
"Assize") were introduced by Jefferson Nov. 25, 1776, and the other
two ("Admiralty" and "County") Dec. 4, 1776. All but the "Admiralty" (which was promptly passed) encountered bitter opposition,
(see note to: Bill for suspending execution for debt, Dec. 6, 1776), and
none were acted upon at this session, nor at the succeeding one. On

On the 12th. I obtained leave to bring in a bill declaring tenants in tail to hold their lands in fee simple.[1] In the earlier times of the colony when lands were to be obtained for little or nothing, some provident individuals procured large grants, and, desirous of founding great families for themselves, settled them on their descendants in fee-tail. The transmission of this property from generation to generation in the same name raised up a distinct set of families who, being privileged by law in the perpetuation of their wealth were thus formed into a Patrician order, distinguished by the splendor and luxury of their establishments. From this order too the king habitually selected his Counsellors of State, the hope of which distinction devoted the whole corps to the interests & will of the crown. To annul this privilege, and instead of an aristocracy of wealth, of more harm and danger, than benefit, to society, to make an opening for the aristocracy of virtue and talent, which nature has wisely provided for the direction of the interests of society, & scattered with equal hand through all it's conditions, was deemed essential to a well ordered republic. To effect it no violence was necessary, no deprivation of natural right, but rather an enlargement of it by a repeal of the law. For this would authorize the present holder to divide the property among his

Oct. 30, 1777, fresh leave was granted to introduce bills establishing Courts of Appeals, "General Court and Court of Assize" and Chancery. The latter two were passed at this session, and the first passed at the first session in 1778. They are all printed in *A Collection of the Public Acts of Virginia.* Richmond, 1785, pp. 66, 70, 84.

[1] See *post*, Oct. 12, 1776.

children equally, as his affections were divided; and
would place them, by natural generation on the level
of their fellow citizens.   But this repeal was strongly
opposed by Mr. Pendleton, who was zealously attached to ancient establishments; and who, taken all
in all, was the ablest man in debate I have ever met
with.   He had not indeed the poetical fancy of Mr.
Henry, his sublime imagination, his lofty and overwhelming diction; but he was cool, smooth and per-
suasive; his language flowing, chaste & embellished,
his conceptions quick, acute and full of resource;
never vanquished; for if he lost the main battle, he
returned upon you, and regained so much of it as to
make it a drawn one, by dexterous manœuvres,
skirmishes in detail, and the recovery of small advantages which, little singly, were important altogether.   You never knew when you were clear of
him, but were harassed by his perseverance until the
patience was worn down of all who had less of it than
himself.   Add to this that he was one of the most
virtuous & benevolent of men, the kindest friend, the
most amiable & pleasant of companions, which en-
sured a favorable reception to whatever came from
him.   Finding that the general principles of entails
could not be maintained, he took his stand on an
amendment which he proposed, instead of an absolute abolition, to permit the tenant in tail to convey
in fee simple, if he chose it: and he was within a few
votes of saving so much of the old law.   But the bill
passed finally for entire abolition.

In that one of the bills for organizing our judiciary
system which proposed a court of chancery, I had

provided for a trial by jury of all matters of fact in that as well as in the courts of law. He defeated it by the introduction of 4. words only, "*if either party chuse.*" [1] The consequence has been that as no suitor will say to his judge, "Sir, I distrust you, give me a jury" juries are rarely, I might say perhaps never seen in that court, but when called for by the Chancellor of his own accord.

The first establishment in Virginia which became permanent was made in 1607. I have found no mention of negroes in the colony until about 1650. The first brought here as slaves were by a Dutch ship; after which the English commenced the trade and continued it until the revolutionary war. That suspended, ipso facto, their further importation for the present, and the business of the war pressing constantly on the legislature, this subject was not acted on finally until the year 78. when I brought in a bill to prevent their further importation.[2] This

---

[1] This was one of the five bills into which the committee by order of the House of Delegates divided the law for the establishment of courts of justice (see *Journal of the House of Delegates*, p. 69). But the original draft of the bill (which is not in Jefferson's handwriting) in the Virginia State Archives contains only the clause concerning juries in the bill as passed, which was to the effect that by mutual agreement of the parties the case could be submitted to the judge, without the calling of a jury, but otherwise a jury trial should be given; such having been the law before the extinction of the courts by the revolutionary conflict. Moreover, with the rough draft of the bill already alluded to, is a separate paper, in Pendleton's handwriting, containing his amendments to the bill, which does not alter in any way the jury system in the original bill.

[2] This is erroneously stated. The earliest step towards this limitation was the permission of the House of Delegates, Nov. 8, 1777, to John Henry and Starke to introduce a bill "to prohibit the importation of slaves." On Nov. 22d, Henry introduced a bill which was read

passed without opposition, and stopped the increase
of the evil by importation, leaving to future efforts
its final eradication.

The first settlers of this colony were Englishmen,
loyal subjects to their king and church, and the grant
to Sr. Walter Raleigh contained an express Proviso
that their laws "should not be against the true
Christian faith, now professed in the church of England." As soon as the state of the colony admitted,
it was divided into parishes, in each of which was
established a minister of the Anglican church, endowed with a fixed salary, in tobacco, a glebe house
and land with the other necessary appendages. To
meet these expenses all the inhabitants of the
parishes were assessed, whether they were or not,
members of the established church. Towards Quak-
ers who came here they were most cruelly intolerant,
driving them from the colony by the severest penal-
ties. In process of time however, other sectarisms
were introduced, chiefly of the Presbyterian family;
and the established clergy, secure for life in their
glebes and salaries, adding to these generally the
emoluments of a classical school, found employment

for a first and second time on that day, and then postponed from time
to time till the end of the session. In the next session, the matter was
taken up *de novo*, on Oct. 15, 1778, by the House of Delegates ordering
the committee of trade to prepare a new bill. It was introduced by
Kella as chairman of the committee on Oct. 15th, passed on Oct. 22d,
amended by the Senate on the 23d, and finally concurred in by the
House, Oct. 27, 1778. Jefferson thus clearly had nothing to do with
the first bill, and, as he did not take his seat at the second session till
Nov. 30th, it is equally certain he had nothing to do with the one which
was adopted.—See *Journal of the House of Delegates* for 1777, pp. 17,
40; for 1778, pp. 11, 13, 19, 23. The original draft of the bill, now in
the Virginia State Archives, is not in Jefferson's handwriting.

enough, in their farms and schoolrooms for the rest of the week, and devoted Sunday only to the edification of their flock, by service, and a sermon at their parish church.   Their other pastoral functions were little attended to.   Against this inactivity the zeal and industry of sectarian preachers had an open and undisputed field; and by the time of the revolution, a majority of the inhabitants had become dissenters from the established church, but were still obliged to pay contributions to support the Pastors of the minority.   This unrighteous compulsion to maintain teachers of what they deemed religious errors was grievously felt during the regal government, and without a hope of relief.   But the first republican legislature which met in 76. was crowded with petitions to abolish this spiritual tyranny.   These brought on the severest contests in which I have ever been engaged.   Our great opponents were Mr. Pendelton & Robert Carter Nicholas, honest men, but zealous churchmen.   The petitions were referred to the commee of the whole house on the state of the country; and after desperate contests in that committee, almost daily from the 11th of Octob.[1] to the 5th of December, we prevailed so far only as to repeal the laws which rendered criminal the maintenance of any religious opinions, the forbearance of repairing to church, or the exercise of any mode of worship: and

[1] An error.   These petitions were invariably referred to the "Committee of Religion" consisting of nineteen members (including Jefferson) appointed Oct. 11, 1776.   See *Journal of the House of Delegates*, pp. 7, 24, 26, 35, 47.   On Nov. 9th, however, that committee was "discharged" of this question and it was referred to the "Committee of the Whole House upon the State of the Country."

further, to exempt dissenters from contributions to the support of the established church; and to suspend, only until the next session levies on the members of that church for the salaries of their own incumbents.   For although the majority of our citizens were dissenters, as has been observed, a majority of the legislature were churchmen.   Among these however were some reasonable and liberal men, who enabled us, on some points, to obtain feeble majorities.   But our opponents carried in the general resolutions of the commee of Nov. 19. a declaration that religious assemblies ought to be regulated, and that provision ought to be made for continuing the succession of the clergy, and superintending their conduct.   And in the bill now passed [1] was inserted an express reservation of the question Whether a general assessment should not be established by law, on every one, to the support of the pastor of his choice; or whether all should be left to voluntary contributions; and on this question, debated at every session from 76 to 79 (some of our dissenting allies, having now secured their particular object, going over to the advocates of a general assessment) we could only obtain a suspension from session to session until 79. when the question against a general assessment was finally carried, and the establishment of the Anglican

[1] Entitled: "An Act for exempting the different societies of dissenters from contributing to the support and maintenance of the church as by law established, and its ministers, and for other purposes therein mentioned."   Passed by the House of Delegates, Dec. 5th. Concurred in by the Senate Dec. 9th.   Re-enacted Jan. 1, 1778.   It is printed in *A Collection of Public Acts of Virginia*, Richmond, 1785, p. 39.

church entirely put down. In justice to the two honest but zealous opponents, who have been named I must add that altho', from their natural temperaments, they were more disposed generally to acquiesce in things as they are, then to risk innovations, yet whenever the public will had once decided, none were more faithful or exact in their obedience to it.

The seat of our government had been originally fixed in the peninsula of Jamestown, the first settlement of the colonists; and had been afterwards removed a few miles inland to Williamsburg. But this was at a time when our settlements had not extended beyond the tide water. Now they had crossed the Alleghany; and the center of population was very far removed from what it had been. Yet Williamsburg was still the depository of our archives, the habitual residence of the Governor & many other of the public functionaries, the established place for the sessions of the legislature, and the magazine of our military stores: and it's situation was so exposed that it might be taken at any time in war, and, at this time particularly, an enemy might in the night run up either of the rivers between which it lies, land a force above, and take possession of the place, without the possibility of saving either persons or things. I had proposed it's removal so early as Octob. 76.[1] but it did not prevail until the session of May. '79.

Early in the session of May 79. I prepared, and obtained leave to bring in a bill declaring who should

[1] This was moved as early as 1761, and only failed by a vote of 35 to 36. A second attempt was made Feb. 10, 1772.—*Journal of the House of Burgesses. Cf. post*, Oct. 14, 1776.

be deemed citizens, asserting the natural right of expatriation, and prescribing the mode of exercising it. This, when I withdrew from the house on the 1st of June following, I left in the hands of George Mason and it was passed on the 26th of that month.[1]

In giving this account of the laws of which I was myself the mover & draughtsman, I by no means mean to claim to myself the merit of obtaining their passage. I had many occasional and strenuous coadjutors in debate, and one most steadfast, able, and zealous; who was himself a host. This was George Mason, a man of the first order of wisdom among those who acted on the theatre of the revolution, of expansive mind, profound judgment, cogent in argument, learned in the lore of our former constitution, and earnest for the republican change on democratic principles. His elocution was neither flowing nor smooth, but his language was strong, his manner most impressive, and strengthened by a dash of biting cynicism when provocation made it seasonable.

Mr. Wythe, while speaker in the two sessions of 1777. between his return from Congress and his appointment to the Chancery, was an able and constant associate in whatever was before a committee of the whole. His pure integrity, judgment and reasoning powers gave him great weight. Of him see more in some notes inclosed in my letter of August 31, 1821, to Mr. John Saunderson.

Mr. Madison came into the House in 1776. a new member and young; which circumstances, concurring

---

[1] Printed in the *Report of the Committee of Revisors*, p. 41.

with his extreme modesty, prevented his ventur-
ing himself in debate before his removal to the
Council of State in Nov. 77. From thence he went to
Congress, then consisting of few members. Trained
in these successive schools, he acquired a habit of
self-possession which placed at ready command the
rich resources of his luminous and discriminating
mind, & of his extensive information, and rendered
him the first of every assembly afterwards of which
he became a member. Never wandering from his
subject into vain declamation, but pursuing it closely
in language pure, classical, and copious, soothing
always the feelings of his adversaries by civilities and
softness of expression, he rose to the eminent station
which he held in the great National convention of
1787. and in that of Virginia which followed, he sustained the new constitution in all its parts, bearing off
the palm against the logic of George Mason, and the
fervid declamation of Mr. Henry. With these con-
summate powers were united a pure and spotless
virtue which no calumny has ever attempted to sully.
Of the powers and polish of his pen, and of the wisdom of his administration in the highest office of the
nation, I need say nothing. They have spoken, and
will forever speak for themselves.

So far we were proceeding in the details of reformation only; selecting points of legislation prominent in
character & principle, urgent, and indicative of the
strength of the general pulse of reformation. When
I left Congress, in 76. it was in the persuasion that
our whole code must be reviewed, adapted to our
republican form of government, and, now that we

had no negatives of Councils, Governors & Kings to restrain us from doing right, that it should be corrected, in all it's parts, with a single eye to reason, & the good of those for whose government it was framed. Early therefore [1] in the session of 76. to which I returned, I moved and presented a bill for the revision of the laws; which was passed on the 24th. of October, and on the 5th. of November Mr. Pendleton, Mr. Wythe, George Mason, Thomas L. Lee and myself were appointed a committee to execute the work. We agreed to meet at Fredericksburg to settle the plan of operation and to distribute the work. We met there accordingly, on the 13th. of January 1777. The first question was whether we should propose to abolish the whole existing system of laws, and prepare a new and complete Institute, or preserve the general system, and only modify it to the present state of things. Mr. Pendleton, contrary to his usual disposition in favor of antient things, was for the former proposition, in which he was joined by Mr. Lee. To this it was objected that to abrogate our whole system would be a bold measure, and probably far beyond the views of the legislature; that they had been in the practice of revising from time to time the laws of the colony, omitting the expired, the repealed and the obsolete, amending only those retained, and probably meant we should now do the same, only including the British statutes as well as our own: that to compose a new Institute like those of Justinian and Bracton, or that of Blackstone, which was the model proposed by Mr. Pendleton, would be an arduous

[1] Oct. 12th. *Cf.* note on this revision, *post*, under June 18, 1779.

undertaking, of vast research, of great consideration
& judgment; and when reduced to a text, every word
of that text, from the imperfection of human language, and it's incompetence to express distinctly
every shade of idea, would become a subject of question & chicanery until settled by repeated adjudications; that this would involve us for ages in
litigation, and render property uncertain until, like
the statutes of old, every word had been tried, and
settled by numerous decisions, and by new volumes
of reports & commentaries; and that no one of us
probably would undertake such a work, which, to be
systematical, must be the work of one hand. This
last was the opinion of Mr. Wythe, Mr. Mason & myself. When we proceeded to the distribution of the
work, Mr. Mason excused himself as, being no lawyer,
he felt himself unqualified for the work, and he
resigned soon after. Mr. Lee excused himself on the
same ground, and died indeed in a short time. The
other two gentlemen therefore and myself divided
the work among us. The common law and statutes
to the 4. James I. (when our separate legislature was
established) were assigned to me; the British statutes
from that period to the present day to Mr. Wythe,
and the Virginia laws to Mr. Pendleton. As the law
of Descents, & the criminal law fell of course within
my portion, I wished the commee to settle the leading principles of these, as a guide for me in framing
them. And with respect to the first, I proposed to
abolish the law of primogeniture, and to make real
estate descendible in parcenary to the next of kin, as
personal property is by the statute of distribution.

Mr. Pendleton wished to preserve the right of primogeniture, but seeing at once that that could not prevail, he proposed we should adopt the Hebrew principle, and give a double portion to the elder son. I observed that if the eldest son could eat twice as much, or do double work, it might be a natural evidence of his right to a double portion; but being on a par in his powers & wants, with his brothers and sisters, he should be on a par also in the partition of the patrimony, and such was the decision of the other members.

On the subject of the Criminal law, all were agreed that the punishment of death should be abolished, except for treason and murder; and that, for other felonies should be substituted hard labor in the public works, and in some cases, the Lex talionis. How this last revolting principle came to obtain our approbation, I do not remember. There remained indeed in our laws a vestige of it in a single case of a slave. it was the English law in the time of the Anglo-Saxons, copied probably from the Hebrew law of "an eye for an eye, a tooth for a tooth," and it was the law of several antient people. But the modern mind had left it far in the rear of it's advances. These points however being settled, we repaired to our respective homes for the preparation of the work.

Feb. 6. In the execution of my part I thought it material not to vary the diction of the antient statutes by modernizing it, nor to give rise to new questions by new expressions. The text of these statutes had been so fully explained and defined by numerous adjudications, as scarcely ever now to produce a question in our courts. I thought it would be useful also, in all new draughts, to reform the style of the later British statutes, and of our own acts of assembly, which from their verbosity, their endless tautologies, their involutions of case within case, and parenthesis within parenthesis, and their multiplied efforts at certainty by *saids* and *aforesaids*, by *ors* and by *ands*, to make them more plain, do really render them more perplexed and incomprehensible, not only to common readers, but to the lawyers themselves. We were employed in this work from that time to Feb. 1779, when we met at Williamsburg, that is to say, Mr. Pendleton, Mr. Wythe & myself, and meeting day by day, we examined critically our several parts, sentence by sentence, scrutinizing and amending until we had agreed on the whole. We then returned home, had fair copies made of our several parts, which were reported to the General Assembly June 18. 1779. by Mr. Wythe and myself, Mr. Pendleton's residence being distant, and he having authorized us by letter to declare his approbation. We had in this work brought so much of the Common law as it was thought necessary to alter, all the British statutes from Magna Charta to the present day, and all the laws of Virginia, from the establishment of our legislature, in the 4th. Jac. 1. to the present time, which we thought should be retained, within the compass of 126 bills, making a printed folio of 90 pages only. Some bills were taken out occasionally, from time to time, and passed; but the main body of the work was not entered on by the legislature until

after the general peace, in 1785. when by the un-
wearied exertions of Mr. Madison, in opposition to the
endless quibbles, chicaneries, perversions, vexations
and delays of lawyers and demi-lawyers, most of
the bills were passed by the legislature, with little
alteration.[1]

The bill for establishing religious freedom,[2] the
principles of which had, to a certain degree, been
enacted before, I had drawn in all the latitude of
reason & right. It still met with opposition; but,
with some mutilations in the preamble, it was finally
passed; and a singular proposition proved that it's
protection of opinion was meant to be universal.
Where the preamble declares that coercion is a departure from the plan of the holy author of our
religion, an amendment was proposed, by inserting
the word "Jesus Christ," so that it should read "a
departure from the plan of Jesus Christ, the holy
author of our religion" the insertion was rejected by
a great majority, in proof that they meant to comprehend, within the mantle of it's protection, the
Jew and the Gentile, the Christian and Mahometan,
the Hindoo, and infidel of every denomination.

Beccaria and other writers on crimes and punishments had satisfied the reasonable world of the
unrightfulness and inefficacy of the punishment of
crimes by death; and hard labor on roads, canals
and other public works, had been suggested as a
proper substitute. The Revisors had adopted these

[1] See *Correspondence of James Madison*, i., 199, 203, 207, 212; iii., 532,
580, 583, 612.
[2] Printed in this edition under June 18, 1779.

opinions; but the general idea of our country had
not yet advanced to that point. The bill therefore
for proportioning crimes and punishments was lost
in the House of Delegates by a majority of a single
vote.¹ I learnt afterwards that the substitute of
hard labor in public was tried (I believe it was in
Pennsylvania) without success. Exhibited as a public spectacle, with shaved heads and mean clothing,
working on the high roads produced in the criminals such a prostration of character, such an abandonment of self-respect, as, instead of reforming, plunged
them into the most desperate & hardened depravity
of morals and character.—To pursue the subject of
this law.—I was written to in 1785 (being then in
Paris) by Directors appointed to superintend the
building of a Capitol in Richmond, to advise them
as to a plan, and to add to it one of a prison. Thinking it a favorable opportunity of introducing into
the state an example of architecture in the classic
style of antiquity, and the Maison quarrée of Nismes,
an antient Roman temple, being considered as the

¹ "We went on slowly but successfully till we arrived at the bill concerning crimes and punishments. Here the adversaries of the Code
exerted their whole force, which, being abetted by the impatience of
its friends in an advanced stage of the session, so far prevailed that the
farther prosecution of the work was postponed till the next session."
—*Madison to Jefferson, January 22, 1786.* "After being altered so as
to remove most of the objections, as was thought [it] was lost by a
single vote. The rage against Horse-stealers had a great influence on
the fate of the bill. Our old bloody code is by this event fully restored."—*Madison to Jefferson, February 15, 1787.* "In the changes
made in the penal law, the Revisors were unfortunately misled into
some of the specious errors of —— [Beccaria] then in the zenith of his
fame as a philosophical legislator."—*Madison to Grimke, January 15,
1828.*

most perfect model existing of what may be called Cubic architecture, I applied to M. Clerissault, who had published drawings of the Antiquities of Nismes, to have me a model of the building made in stucco, only changing the order from Corinthian to Ionic, on account of the difficulty of the Corinthian capitals. I yielded with reluctance to the taste of Clerissault, in his preference of the modern capital of Scamozzi to the more noble capital of antiquity. This was executed by the artist whom Choiseul Gouffier had carried with him to Constantinople, and employed while Ambassador there, in making those beautiful models of the remains of Grecian architecture which are to be seen at Paris. To adapt the exterior to our use, I drew a plan for the interior, with the apartments necessary for legislative, executive & judiciary purposes, and accommodated in their size and distribution to the form and dimensions of the building. These were forwarded to the Directors in 1786. and were carried into execution, with some variations not for the better, the most important of which however admit of future correction. With respect to the plan of a Prison, requested at the same time, I had heard of a benevolent society in England which had been indulged by the government in an experiment of the effect of labor in *solitary confinement* on some of their criminals, which experiment had succeeded beyond expectation. The same idea had been suggested in France, and an Architect of Lyons had proposed a plan of a well contrived edifice on the principle of solitary confinement. I procured a copy, and as it was too large for our purposes, I drew one on a scale, less extensive, but susceptible of additions as they should be wanting. This I sent to the Directors instead of a plan of a common prison, in the hope that it would suggest the idea of labor in solitary confinement instead of that on the public works, which we had adopted in our Revised Code. It's principle accordingly, but not it's exact form, was adopted by Latrobe in carrying the plan into execution, by the erection of what is now called the Penitentiary, built under his direction. In the meanwhile the public opinion was ripening by time, by reflection, and by the example of Pensylva, where labor on the highways had been tried without approbation from 1786 to 89. & had been followed by their Penitentiary system on the principle of confinement and labor, which was proceeding auspiciously. In 1796. our legislature resumed the subject and passed the law for amending the Penal laws of the commonwealth. They adopted solitary, instead of public labor, established a gradation in the duration of the confinement, approximated the style of the law more to the modern usage, and instead of the settled distinctions of murder & manslaughter, preserved in my bill, they introduced the new terms of murder in the 1st & 2d degree. Whether these have produced more or fewer questions of definition I am not sufficiently informed of our judiciary transactions to say. I will here however insert the text of my bill, with the notes I made in the course of my researches into the subject.[1]

[1] Printed in this edition under June 18, 1779.

Feb. 7. The acts of assembly concerning the College of Wm. & Mary, were properly within Mr. Pendleton's portion of our work. But these related chiefly to it's revenue, while it's constitution, organization and scope of science were derived from it's charter. We thought, that on this subject a systematical plan of general education should be proposed, and I was requested to undertake it. I accordingly prepared three bills for the Revisal, proposing three distinct grades of education, reaching all classes.[1] 1. Elementary schools for all children generally, rich and poor. 2. Colleges for a middle degree of instruction, calculated for the common purposes of life, and such as would be desirable for all who were in easy circumstances. And 3d. an ultimate grade for teaching the sciences generally, & in their highest degree. The first bill proposed to lay off every county into Hundreds or Wards, of a proper size and population for a school, in which reading, writing, and common arithmetic should be taught; and that the whole state should be divided into 24 districts, in each of which should be a school for classical learning, grammar, geography, and the higher branches of numerical arithmetic. The second bill proposed to amend the constitution of Wm. & Mary College, to enlarge it's sphere of science, and to make it in fact an University. The third was for the establishment of a library. These bills were not acted on until the same year '96. and then only so much of the first as provided for elementary schools. The College of Wm. & Mary was an establishment

[1] Printed in this edition under June 18, 1779.

purely of the Church of England, the Visitors were required to be all of that Church; the Professors to subscribe it's 39 Articles, it's Students to learn it's Catechism, and one of its fundamental objects was declared to be to raise up Ministers for that church. The religious jealousies therefore of all the dissenters took alarm lest this might give an ascendancy to the Anglican sect and refused acting on that bill. Its local eccentricity too and unhealthy autumnal climate lessened the general inclination towards it. And in the Elementary bill they inserted a provision which completely defeated it, for they left it to the court of each county to determine for itself when this act should be carried into execution, within their county. One provision of the bill was that the expenses of these schools should be borne by the inhabitants of the county, every one in proportion to his general tax-rate. This would throw on wealth the education of the poor; and the justices, being generally of the more wealthy class, were unwilling to incur that burthen, and I believe it was not suffered to commence in a single county. I shall recur again to this subject towards the close of my story, if I should have life and resolution enough to reach that term; for I am already tired of talking about myself.

The bill on the subject of slaves was a mere digest of the existing laws respecting them, without any intimation of a plan for a future & general emancipation. It was thought better that this should be kept back, and attempted only by way of amendment whenever the bill should be brought on.[1]   The prin-

[1] *Cf. post*, with *Notes on Virginia* in this edition.

ciples of the amendment however were agreed on,
that is to say, the freedom of all born after a certain
day, and deportation at a proper age.   But it was
found that the public mind would not yet bear the
proposition, nor will it bear it even at this day.   Yet
the day is not distant when it must bear and adopt
it, or worse will follow.   Nothing is more certainly
written in the book of fate than that these people
are to be free.   Nor is it less certain that the two
races, equally free, cannot live in the same government.   Nature, habit, opinion has drawn indelible
lines of distinction between them.   It is still in our
power to direct the process of emancipation and deportation peaceably and in such slow degree as that
the evil will wear off insensibly, and their place be
pari passu filled up by free white laborers.   If on the
contrary it is left to force itself on, human nature
must shudder at the prospect held up.   We should
in vain look for an example in the Spanish deportation or deletion of the Moors.   This precedent would
fall far short of our case.

I considered 4 of these bills, passed or reported,
as forming a system by which every fibre would be
eradicated of antient or future aristocracy; and a
foundation laid for a government truly republican.
The repeal of the laws of entail would prevent the
accumulation and perpetuation of wealth in select
families, and preserve the soil of the country from
being daily more & more absorbed in Mortmain.
The abolition of primogeniture, and equal partition
of inheritances removed the feudal and unnatural
distinctions which made one member of every family

rich, and all the rest poor, substituting equal partition, the best of all Agrarian laws. The restoration of the rights of conscience relieved the people from taxation for the support of a religion not theirs; for the establishment was truly of the religion of the rich, the dissenting sects being entirely composed of the less wealthy people; and these, by the bill for a general education, would be qualified to understand their rights, to maintain them, and to exercise with intelligence their parts in self-government: and all this would be effected without the violation of a single natural right of any one individual citizen.   To these too might be added, as a further security, the introduction of the trial by jury, into the Chancery courts, which have already ingulfed and continue to ingulf, so great a proportion of the jurisdiction over our property.

On the 1st of June 1779. I was appointed Governor of the Commonwealth and retired from the legislature. Being elected also one of the Visitors of Wm. & Mary college, a self-electing body, I effected, during my residence in Williamsburg that year, a change in the organization of that institution by abolishing the Grammar school, and the two professorships of Divinity & Oriental languages, and substituting a professorship of Law & Police, one of Anatomy Medicine and Chemistry, and one of Modern languages; and the charter confining us to six professorships,[1] we added the law of Nature & Nations, & the Fine Arts to the duties of the Moral professor, and Natural history to those of the professor of Mathematics and Natural philosophy.

[1] *Cf. post*, with *Notes on Virginia* in this edition.

Being now, as it were, identified with the Commonwealth itself, to write my own history during the two years of my administration, would be to write the public history of that portion of the revolution within this state. This has been done by others, and particularly by Mr. Girardin, who wrote his Continuation of Burke's history of Virginia while at Milton, in this neighborhood, had free access to all my papers while composing it, and has given as faithful an account as I could myself. For this portion therefore of my own life, I refer altogether to his history. From a belief that under the pressure of the invasion under which we were then laboring the public would have more confidence in a Military chief, and that the Military commander, being invested with the Civil power also, both might be wielded with more energy promptitude and effect for the defence of the state, I resigned the administration at the end of my 2d. year, and General Nelson was appointed to succeed me.

Soon after my leaving Congress in Sep. '76, to wit on the last day of that month,[1] I had been appointed, with Dr. Franklin, to go to France, as a Commissioner to negotiate treaties of alliance and commerce with that government. Silas Deane, then in France, acting as agent [2] for procuring military stores, was

---

[1] An error. He was appointed Sept. 26th.—*Secret Journals of Congress*, ii., 31.

[2] His ostensible character was to be that of a merchant, his real one that of agent for military supplies, and also for sounding the dispositions of the government of France, and seeing how far they would favor us, either secretly or openly. His appointment had been by the Committee of Foreign Correspondence, March, 1776.—*T. J.*

joined with us in commission. But such was the
state of my family that I could not leave it, nor
could I expose it to the dangers of the sea, and of
capture by the British ships, then covering the
ocean. I saw too that the laboring oar was really
at home, where much was to be done of the most
permanent interest in new modelling our governments, and much to defend our fanes and fire-sides
from the desolations of an invading enemy pressing
on our country in every point. I declined therefore
and Dr. Lee was appointed in my place. On the
15th. of June [1] 1781. I had been appointed with Mr.
Adams, Dr. Franklin, Mr. Jay, and Mr. Laurens a
Minister plenipotentiary for negotiating peace, then
expected to be effected thro' the mediation of the
Empress of Russia. The same reasons obliged me
still to decline; and the negotiation was in fact
never entered on. But, in the autumn of the next
year 1782 Congress receiving assurances that a general peace would be concluded in the winter and
spring, they renewed my appointment on the 13th.
of Nov. of that year. I had two months before that
lost the cherished companion of my life, in whose
affections, unabated on both sides I had lived the
last ten years in unchequered happiness. With the
public interests, the state of my mind concurred in
recommending the change of scene proposed; and
I accepted the appointment, and left Monticello on
the 19th. of Dec. 1782. for Philadelphia, where I
arrived on the 27th. The Minister of France, Luzerne, offered me a passage in the *Romulus* frigate,

---

[1] By the *Secret Journal of Congress* it was June 14th.

which I accepting.   But she was then lying a few miles below Baltimore blocked up in the ice.   I remained therefore a month in Philadelphia, looking over the papers in the office of State in order to possess myself of the general state of our foreign relations, and then went to Baltimore to await the liberation of the frigate from the ice.   After waiting there nearly a month, we received information that a Provisional treaty of peace had been signed by our Commissioners on the 3d. of Sep. 1782. to become absolute on the conclusion of peace between France and Great Britain.   Considering my proceeding to Europe as now of no utility to the public, I returned immediately to Philadelphia to take the orders of Congress, and was excused by them from further proceeding.   I therefore returned home, where I arrived on the 15th. of May, 1783.

On the 6th. of the following month I was appointed by the legislature a delegate to Congress, the appointment to take place on the 1st. of Nov. ensuing, when that of the existing delegation would expire.   I accordingly left home on the 16th. of Oct. arrived at Trenton, where Congress was sitting, on the 3d. of Nov. and took my seat on the 4th., on which day Congress adjourned to meet at Annapolis on the 26th.

Congress had now become a very small body, and the members very remiss in their attendance on it's duties insomuch that a majority of the states, necessary by the Confederation to constitute a house even for minor business did not assemble until the 13th. of December.

They as early as Jan. 7. 1782. had turned their

attention to the monies current in the several states, and had directed the Financier, Robert Morris, to report to them a table of rates at which the foreign coins should be received at the treasury. That officer, or rather his assistant, Gouverneur Morris, answered them on the 15th [1] in an able and elaborate statement of the denominations of money current in the several states, and of the comparative value of the foreign coins chiefly in circulation with us. He went into the consideration of the necessity of establishing a standard of value with us, and of the adoption of a money-Unit. He proposed for the Unit such a fraction of pure silver as would be a common measure of the penny of every state, without leaving a fraction. This common divisor he found to be 1–1440 of a dollar, or 1–1600 of the crown sterling. The value of a dollar was therefore to be expressed by 1440 units, and of a crown by 1600. Each unit containing a quarter of a grain of fine silver. Congress turning again their attention to this subject the following year, the financier, by a letter of Apr. 30, 1783. further explained and urged the Unit he had proposed; but nothing more was done on it until the ensuing year, when it was again taken up, and referred to a commee of which I was a member. The general views of the financier were sound, and the principle was ingenious on which he proposed to found his Unit. But it was too minute for ordinary use, too laborious for computation either by the head or in figures. The price of a loaf of bread 1–20 of a dollar would be 72. units.

[1] *Diplomatic Correspondence*, xii., 81.

A pound of butter 1–5 of a dollar 288. units.

A horse or bullock of 80. D value would require a notation of 6. figures, to wit 115,200, and the public debt, suppose of 80. millions, would require 12. figures, to wit 115,200,000,000 units. Such a system of money-arithmetic would be entirely unmanageable for the common purposes of society. I proposed therefore, instead of this, to adopt the Dollar as our Unit of account and payment, and that it's divisions and sub-divisions should be in the decimal ratio. I wrote some Notes [1] on the subject, which I submitted to the consideration of the financier. I received his answer and adherence to his general system, only agreeing to take for his Unit 100. of those he first proposed, so that a Dollar should be 14 40–100 and a crown 16. units. I replied to this and printed my notes and reply on a flying sheet, which I put into the hands of the members of Congress for consideration, and the Committee agreed to report on my principle. This was adopted the ensuing year and is the system which now prevails. I insert here the Notes and Reply, as shewing the different views on which the adoption of our money system hung. The division into dimes, cents & mills is now so well understood, that it would be easy of introduction into the kindred branches of weights & measures. I use, when I travel, an Odometer of Clarke's invention which divides the mile into cents, and I find every one comprehend a distance readily when stated to them in miles & cents; so they would in feet and cents, pounds & cents, &c.

[1] Printed in this edition under 1784.

The remissness of Congress, and their permanent session, began to be a subject of uneasiness and even some of the legislatures had recommended to them intermissions, and periodical sessions. As the Confederation had made no provision for a visible head of the government during vacations of Congress, and such a one was necessary to superintend the executive business, to receive and communicate with foreign ministers & nations, and to assemble Congress on sudden and extraordinary emergencies, I proposed early in April [1] the appointment of a commee to be called the Committee of the states, to consist of a member from each state, who should remain in session during the recess of Congress: that the functions of Congress should be divided into Executive and Legislative, the latter to be reserved, and the former, by a general resolution to be delegated to that Committee. This proposition was afterwards agreed to; a Committee appointed, who entered on duty on the subsequent adjournment of Congress, quarrelled very soon, split into two parties, abandoned their post and left the government without any visible head until the next meeting in Congress. We have since seen the same thing take place in the Directory of France; and I believe it will forever take place in any Executive consisting of a plurality. Our plan, best I believe, combines wisdom and practicability, by providing a plurality of Counsellors, but a single Arbiter for ultimate decision. I was in France when we heard of this schism,

[1] April 14, 1784. *Journal of Congress*, ix., 127. *Cf. post*, under Jan. 30, 1784, Jefferson's report on the committee of the States.

and separation of our Committee, and, speaking
with Dr. Franklin of this singular disposition of men
to quarrel and divide into parties, he gave his sentiments as usual by way of Apologue. He mentioned
the Eddystone lighthouse in the British channel as
being built on a rock in the mid-channel, totally in-
accessible in winter, from the boisterous character
of that sea, in that season. That therefore, for the
two keepers employed to keep up the lights, all provisions for the winter were necessarily carried to
them in autumn, as they could never be visited again
till the return of the milder season. That on the
first practicable day in the spring a boat put off to
them with fresh supplies. The boatmen met at the
door one of the keepers and accosted him with a How
goes it friend? Very well. How is your companion?
I do not know. Don't know? Is not he here? I can't
tell. Have not you seen him to-day? No. When did
you see him? Not since last fall. You have killed
him? Not I, indeed. They were about to lay hold
of him, as having certainly murdered his companion;
but he desired them to go up stairs & examine for
themselves. They went up, and there found the
other keeper. They had quarrelled it seems soon after
being left there, had divided into two parties, assigned
the cares below to one, and those above to the other,
and had never spoken to or seen one another since.

But to return to our Congress at Annapolis, the
definitive treaty of peace which had been signed at
Paris on the 3d. of Sep. 1783. and received here,
could not be ratified without a House of 9. states.[1]

[1] Cf. post, under Jan., 1784.

On the 23d. of Dec.[1] therefore we addressed letters
to the several governors, stating the receipt of the
definitive treaty, that 7 states only were in attendance, while 9. were necessary to its ratification, and
urging them to press on their delegates the necessity
of their immediate attendance.   And on the 26th.
to save time I moved that the Agent of Marine (Robert Morris) should be instructed to have ready a
vessel at this place, at N. York, & at some Eastern
port, to carry over the ratification of the treaty when
agreed to.   It met the general sense of the house,
but was opposed by Dr. Lee [2] on the ground of expense which it would authorize the agent to incur for
us; and he said it would be better to ratify at once
& send on the ratification.   Some members had
before suggested that 7 states were competent to the
ratification.   My motion was therefore postponed
and another brought forward by Mr. Read [3] of S. C.
for an immediate ratification.   This was debated
the 26th. and 27th.   Reed, Lee, [Hugh] Williamson
& Jeremiah Chace urged that ratification was a
mere matter of form, that the treaty was conclusive
from the moment it was signed by the ministers;
that although the Confederation requires the assent
of 9. *states* to *enter into* a treaty, yet that it's conclusion could not be called *entrance into it;* that sup-
posing 9. states requisite, it would be in the power
of 5. states to keep us always at war; that 9. states
had virtually authorized the ratifion having ratified

[1] On motion of Williamson, seconded by **Jefferson.**
[2] Arthur Lee, Delegate from Virginia.
[3] Jacob Read.

the provisional treaty, and instructed their ministers
to agree to a definitive one in the same terms, and
the present one was in fact substantially and almost
verbatim the same; that there now remain but 67.
days for the ratification, for it's passage across the
Atlantic, and it's exchange; that there was no hope
of our soon having 9. states present; in fact that this
was the ultimate point of time to which we could
venture to wait; that if the ratification was not in
Paris by the time stipulated, the treaty would become void; that if ratified by 7 states, it would go
under our seal without it's being known to Gr.
Britain that only 7. had concurred; that it was a
question of which they had no right to take cogni-
zance, and we were only answerable for it to our
constituents; that it was like the ratification which
Gr. Britain had received from the Dutch by the
negotiations of Sr. Wm. Temple.

On the contrary, it was argued by Monroe, Gerry,
Howel, Ellery & myself that by the modern usage
of Europe the ratification was considered as the act
which gave validity to a treaty, until which it was
not obligatory.[1]   That the commission to the ministers reserved the ratification to Congress; that the
treaty itself stipulated that it should be ratified;
that it became a 2d. question who were competent
to the ratification? That the Confederation expressly required 9 states to enter into any treaty;
that, by this, that instrument must have intended
that the assent of 9. states should be necessary as

[1] Vattel, L. 2, § 156.   L. 4, § 77.   1. Mably Droit D'Europe, 86.—
T. J.

well to the *completion* as to the *commencement* of the
treaty, it's object having been to guard the rights
of the Union in all those important cases where 9.
states are called for; that, by the contrary con-
struction, 7 states, containing less than one third of
our whole citizens, might rivet on us a treaty, commenced indeed under commission and instructions
from 9. states, but formed by the minister in express contradiction to such instructions, and in
direct sacrifice of the interests of so great a majority; that the definitive treaty was admitted not
to be a verbal copy of the provisional one, and
whether the departures from it were of substance
or not, was a question on which 9. states alone were
competent to decide; that the circumstances of the
ratification of the provisional articles by 9. states the
instructions to our ministers to form a definitive one
by them, and their actual agreement in substance,
do not render us competent to ratify in the present
instance; if these circumstances are in themselves a
ratification, nothing further is requisite than to give
attested copies of them, in exchange for the British
ratification; if they are not, we remain where we
were, without a ratification by 9. states, and incom-
petent ourselves to ratify; that it was but 4. days
since the seven states now present unanimously concurred in a resolution to be forwarded to the governors of the absent states, in which they stated as a
cause for urging on their delegates, that 9. states
were necessary to ratify the treaty; that in the case
of the Dutch ratification, Gr. Britain had courted it,
and therefore was glad to accept it as it was; that

they knew our constitution, and would object to a
ratification by 7. that if that circumstance was kept
back, it would be known hereafter, & would give
them ground to deny the validity of a ratification
into which they should have been surprised and
cheated, and it would be a dishonorable prostitution
of our seal; that there is a hope of 9. states; that
if the treaty would become null if not ratified in
time, it would not be saved by an imperfect ratification; but that in fact it would not be null, and would
be placed on better ground, going in unexceptionable
form, tho' a few days too late, and rested on the
small importance of this circumstance, and the physical impossibilities which had prevented a punctual
compliance in point of time; that this would be approved by all nations, & by Great Britain herself, if
not determined to renew the war, and if determined,
she would never want excuses, were this out of the
way.   Mr. Reade gave notice he should call for the
yeas & nays; whereon those in opposition prepared
a resolution expressing pointedly the reasons of the
dissent from his motion.   It appearing however that
his proposition could not be carried, it was thought
better to make no entry at all.   Massachusetts
alone would have been for it; Rhode Island, Pennsylvania and Virginia against it, Delaware, Maryland & N. Carolina, would have been divided.

Our body was little numerous, but very conten-
tious.   Day after day was wasted on the most un-
important questions.   My colleague Mercer [1] was
one of those afflicted with the morbid rage of debate,

[1] John F. Mercer.

of an ardent mind, prompt imagination, and copious
flow of words, he heard with impatience any logic
which was not his own. Sitting near me on some
occasion of a trifling but wordy debate, he asked how
I could sit in silence hearing so much false reasoning
which a word should refute?   I observed to him that
to refute indeed was easy, but to silence impossible.
That in measures brought forward by myself, I took
the laboring oar, as was incumbent on me; but that
in general I was willing to listen. If every sound
argument or objection was used by some one or other
of the numerous debaters, it was enough: if not, I
thought it sufficient to suggest the omission, without
going into a repetition of what had been already said
by others.   That this was a waste and abuse of the
time and patience of the house which could not be
justified.   And I believe that if the members of de-
liberative bodies were to observe this course generally, they would do in a day what takes them a week,
and it is really more questionable, than may at first
be thought, whether Bonaparte's dumb legislature
which said nothing and did much, may not be pre-
ferable to one which talks much and does nothing. I
served with General Washington in the legislature of
Virginia before the revolution, and, during it, with
Dr. Franklin in Congress.   I never heard either of
them speak ten minutes at a time, nor to any but
the main point which was to decide the question.
They laid their shoulders to the great points, knowing that the little ones would follow of themselves.
If the present Congress errs in too much talking, how
can it be otherwise in a body to which the people

send 150. lawyers, whose trade it is to question everything, yield nothing, & talk by the hour? That 150.
lawyers should do business together ought not to be
expected.   But to return again to our subject.

Those who thought 7. states competent to the
ratification being very restless under the loss of their
motion, I proposed, on the 3d. of January to meet
them on middle ground, and therefore moved a resolution ¹ which premising that there were but 7. states
present, who were unanimous for the ratification,
but, that they differed in opinion on the question
of competency.   That those however in the negative
were unwilling that any powers which it might be supposed they possessed should remain unexercised for
the restoration of peace, provided it could be done
saving their good faith, and without importing any
opinion of Congress that 7. states were competent,
and resolving that treaty be ratified so far as they
had power; that it should be transmitted to our
ministers with instructions to keep it uncommuni-
cated; to endeavor to obtain 3. months longer for
exchange of ratifications; that they should be informed that so soon as 9. states shall be present a
ratification by 9. shall be sent them; if this should
get to them before the ultimate point of time for exchange, they were to use it, and not the other; if
not, they were to offer the act of the 7. states in exchange, informing them the treaty had come to
hand while Congress was not in session, that but 7.
states were as yet assembled, and these had unanimously concurred in the ratification.   This was

¹ Printed in this edition under that date.

debated on the 3d. and 4th.[1] and on the 5th. a vessel being to sail for England from this port (Annapolis) the House directed the President to write to our ministers accordingly.

Jan. 14. Delegates from Connecticut having attended yesterday, and another from S. Carolina coming in this day, the treaty was ratified without a dissenting voice, and three instruments of ratification were ordered to be made out, one of which was sent by Colo. Harmer, another by Colo. Franks, and the 3d. transmitted to the agent of Marine to be forwarded by any good opportunity.

Congress soon took up the consideration of their foreign relations. They deemed it necessary to get their commerce placed with every nation on a footing as favorable as that of other nations; and for this purpose to propose to each a distinct treaty of commerce. This act too would amount to an acknowledgment by each of our independance and of our reception into the fraternity of nations; which altho', as possessing our station of right and in fact, we would not condescend to ask, we were not unwilling to furnish opportunities for receiving their friendly salutations & welcome. With France the United Netherlands and Sweden we had already treaties of commerce, but commissions were given for those countries also, should any amendments be thought necessary. The other states to which treaties were to be proposed were England, Hamburg, Saxony, Prussia, Denmark, Russia, Austria, Venice, Rome, Naples, Tuscany, Sardinia, Genoa,

[1] The 4th of January, 1784, was Sunday, so Congress did not sit.

Spain, Portugal, the Porte, Algiers, Tripoli, Tunis & Morocco.[1]

Mar. 16. On the 7th. of May Congress resolved that a Minister Plenipotentiary should be appointed in addition to Mr. Adams & Dr. Franklin for negotiating treaties of commerce with foreign nations, and I was elected to that duty. I accordingly left Annapolis on the 11th. Took with me my elder daughter[2] then at Philadelphia (the two others being too young for the voyage) & proceeded to Boston in quest of a passage. While passing thro' the different states, I made a point of informing myself of the state of the commerce of each, went on to New Hampshire with the same view and returned to Boston. From thence I sailed on the 5th. of July in the *Ceres* a merchant ship of Mr. Nathaniel Tracey, bound to Cowes. He was himself a passenger, and, after a pleasant voyage of 19. days from land to land, we arrived at Cowes on the 26th. I was detained there a few days by the indisposition of my daughter. On the 30th. we embarked for Havre, arrived there on the 31st. left it on the 3d. of August, and arrived at Paris on the 6th. I called immediately on Doctr. Franklin at Passy, communicated to him our charge, and we wrote to Mr. Adams, then at the Hague to join us at Paris.

Before I had left America, that is to say in the year 1781. I had received a letter from M. de Marbois, of the French legation in Philadelphia, informing me he had been instructed by his government to

---

[1] See Jefferson's report on European treaties, *post*, under 1784.
[2] Martha Jefferson, afterwards Mrs. Thomas Mann Randolph.

obtain such statistical accounts of the different states of our Union, as might be useful for their information; and addressing to me a number of queries relative to the state of Virginia.   I had always made it a practice whenever an opportunity occurred of obtaining any information of our country, which might be of use to me in any station public or private, to commit it to writing.   These memoranda were on loose papers, bundled up without order, and difficult of recurrence when I had occasion for a particular one.   I thought this a good occasion to embody their substance, which I did in the order of Mr. Marbois' queries, so as to answer his wish and to arrange them for my own use.   Some friends to whom they were occasionally communicated wished for copies; but their volume rendering this too laborious by hand, I proposed to get a few printed for their gratification.   I was asked such a price however as exceeded the importance of the object. On my arrival at Paris I found it could be done for a fourth of what I had been asked here.   I therefore corrected and enlarged them, and had 200. copies printed, under the title of *Notes on Virginia.* I gave a very few copies to some particular persons in Europe, and sent the rest to my friends in America. An European copy, by the death of the owner, got into the hands of a bookseller, who engaged it's translation, & when ready for the press, communicated his intentions & manuscript to me, without any other permission than that of suggesting corrections.   I never had seen so wretched an attempt at translation.   Interverted, abridged, mutilated, and often reversing the sense of the original, I found it a blotch of errors from beginning to end. I corrected some of the most material, and in that form it was printed in French.[1] A London bookseller, on seeing the translation, requested me to permit him to print the English original. I thought it best to do so to let the world see that it was not really so bad as the French translation had made it appear. And this is the true history of that publication.

Mr. Adams soon joined us at Paris, & our first employment was to prepare a general form to be proposed to such nations as were disposed to treat with us. During the negotiations for peace with the British Commissioner David Hartley, our Commissioners had proposed, on the suggestion of Doctr. Franklin, to insert an article exempting from capture by the public or private armed ships of either belligerent, when at war, all merchant vessels and their cargoes, employed merely in carrying on the commerce between nations. It was refused by England, and unwisely, in my opinion. For in the case of a war with us, their superior commerce places infinitely more at hazard on the ocean than ours; and as hawks abound in proportion to game, so our privateers would swarm in proportion to the wealth exposed to their prize, while theirs would be few for want of subjects of capture. We inserted this article in our form, with a provision against the molestation of fishermen, husbandmen, citizens unarmed and following their occupations in unfortified places, for the humane treatment of prisoners of war,

[1] Cf. *post*, note on *Notes on Virginia* under 1782.

the abolition of contraband of war, which exposes merchant vessels to such vexatious & ruinous detentions and abuses; and for the principle of free bottoms, free goods.

In a conference with the Count de Vergennes, it was thought better to leave to legislative regulation on both sides such modifications of our commercial intercourse as would voluntarily flow from amicable dispositions. Without urging, we sounded the ministers of the several European nations at the court of Versailles, on their dispositions towards mutual commerce, and the expediency of encouraging it by the protection of a treaty. Old Frederic of Prussia met us cordially and without hesitation, and appointing the Baron de Thulemeyer, his minister at the Hague, to negotiate with us, we communicated to him our Project, which with little alteration by the King, was soon concluded. Denmark and Tuscany entered also into negotiations with us. Other powers appearing indifferent we did not think it proper to press them. They seemed in fact to know little about us, but as rebels who had been successful in throwing off the yoke of the mother country. They were ignorant of our commerce, which had been always monopolized by England, and of the exchange of articles it might offer advantageously to both parties. They were inclined therefore to stand aloof until they could see better what relations might be usefully instituted with us. The negotiations therefore begun with Denmark & Tuscany we protracted designedly until our powers had expired; and abstained from making new propositions to others having no colonies; because our commerce being an exchange of raw for wrought materials, is a competent price for admission into the colonies of those possessing them: but were we to give it, without price, to others, all would claim it without price on the ordinary ground of gentis amicissimæ.

Mr. Adams being appointed Min. Pleny. of the U S. to London, left us in June, and in July 1785. Dr. Franklin returned to America, and I was appointed his successor at Paris. In Feb. 1786. Mr. Adams wrote to me pressingly to join him in London immediately, as he thought he discovered there some symptoms of better disposition towards us. Colo. Smith,[1] his Secretary of legation, was the bearer of his urgencies for my immediate attendance. I accordingly left Paris on the 1st. of March, and on my arrival in London we agreed on a very summary form of treaty, proposing an exchange of citizenship for our citizens, our ships, and our productions generally, except as to office. On my presentation as usual to the King and Queen at their levées, it was impossible for anything to be more ungracious than their notice of Mr. Adams & myself. I saw at once that the ulcerations in the narrow mind of that mulish being left nothing to be expected on the subject of my attendance; and on the first conference with the Marquis of Caermarthen, his Minister of foreign affairs, the distance and disinclination which he betrayed in his conversation, the vagueness & evasions of his answers to us, confirmed me in the belief of their aversion to have anything to do with us. We

[1] William Stephens Smith.

delivered him however our Projét, Mr. Adams not despairing as much as I did of it's effect.   We afterwards, by one or more notes, requested his appointment of an interview and conference, which, without directly declining, he evaded by pretences of other pressing occupations for the moment.   After staying there seven weeks, till within a few days of the expiration of our commission, I informed the minister by note that my duties at Paris required my return to that place, and that I should with pleasure be the bearer of any commands to his Ambassador there. He answered that he had none, and wishing me a pleasant journey, I left London the 26th. arrived at Paris on the 30th. of April.

While in London we entered into negotiations with the Chevalier Pinto, Ambassador of Portugal at that place.   The only article of difficulty between us was a stipulation that our bread stuff should be received in Portugal in the form of flour as well as of grain.   He approved of it himself, but observed that several Nobles, of great influence at their court, were the owners of wind mills in the neighborhood of Lisbon which depended much for their profits on manufacturing our wheat, and that this stipulation would endanger the whole treaty.   He signed it however, & it's fate was what he had candidly portended.

My duties at Paris were confined to a few objects; the receipt of our whale-oils, salted fish, and salted meats on favorable terms, the admission of our rice on equal terms with that of Piedmont, Egypt & the Levant, a mitigation of the monopolies of our tobacco by the Farmers-general, and a free admission of our

productions into their islands; were the principal
commercial objects which required attention; and
on these occasions I was powerfully aided by all the
influence and the energies of the Marquis de La
Fayette, who proved himself equally zealous for the
friendship and welfare of both nations; and in justice I must also say that I found the government
entirely disposed to befriend us on all occasions, and
to yield us every indulgence not absolutely injurious
to themselves. The Count de Vergennes had the
reputation with the diplomatic corps of being wary
& slippery in his diplomatic intercourse; and so he
might be with those whom he knew to be slippery
and double-faced themselves. As he saw that I had
no indirect views, practised no subtleties, meddled
in no intrigues, pursued no concealed object, I found
him as frank, as honorable, as easy of access to
reason as any man with whom I had ever done
business; and I must say the same for his successor
Montmorin, one of the most honest and worthy of
human beings.

Our commerce in the Mediterranean was placed
under early alarm by the capture of two of our vessels and crews by the Barbary cruisers. I was very
unwilling that we should acquiesce in the European
humiliation of paying a tribute to those lawless
pirates, and endeavored to form an association of
the powers subject to habitual depredation from
them. I accordingly prepared and proposed to
their ministers at Paris, for consultation with their
governments, articles of a special confederation in
the following form.

Proposals for concerted operation among the powers at war with the Piratical States of Barbary.

" 1. It is proposed that the several powers at war with the Piratical States of Barbary, or any two or more of them who shall be willing, shall enter into a convention to carry on their operations against those states, in concert, beginning with the Algerines.

" 2. This convention shall remain open to any other power who shall at any future time wish to accede to it; · the parties reserving a right to prescribe the conditions of such accession, according to the circumstances existing at the time it shall be proposed.

" 3. The object of the convention shall be to compel the piratical states to perpetual peace, without price, & to guarantee that peace to each other.

" 4. The operations for obtaining this peace shall be constant cruises on their coast with a naval force now to be agreed on. It is not proposed that this force shall be so considerable as to be inconvenient to any party. It is believed that half a dozen frigates, with as many Tenders or Xebecs, one half of which shall be in cruise, while the other half is at rest, will suffice.

" 5. The force agreed to be necessary shall be furnished by the parties in certain quotas now to be fixed; it being expected that each will be willing to contribute in such proportion as circumstance may render reasonable.

" 6. As miscarriages often proceed from the want of harmony among officers of different nations, the parties shall now consider & decide whether it will not be better to contribute their quotas in money to be employed in fitting out, and keeping on duty, a single fleet of the force agreed on.

"7. The difficulties and delays too which will attend the management of these operations, if conducted by the parties themselves separately, distant as their courts may be from one another, and incapable of meeting in consultation, suggest a question whether it will not be better for them to give full powers for that purpose to their Ambassadors or other ministers resident at some one court of Europe, who shall form a Committee or Council for carrying this convention into effect; wherein the vote of each member shall be computed in proportion to the quota of his sovereign, and the majority so computed shall prevail in all questions within the view of this convention. The court of Versailles is proposed, on account of it's neighborhood to the Mediterranean, and because all those powers are represented there, who are likely to become parties to this convention.

"8. To save to that council the embarrassment of personal solicitations for office, and to assure the parties that their contributions will be applied solely to the object for which they are destined, there shall be no establishment of officers for the said Council, such as Commis, Secretaries, or any other kind, with either salaries or perquisites, nor any other lucrative appointments but such whose functions are to be exercised on board the sd vessels.

"9. Should war arise between any two of the parties to this convention it shall not extend to this enterprise, nor interrupt it; but as to this they shall be reputed at peace.

" 10. When Algiers shall be reduced to peace, the other pyratical states, if they refuse to discontinue their pyracies shall become the objects of this convention, either successively or together as shall seem best.

" 11. Where this convention would interfere with treaties actually existing between any of the parties and the sd states of Barbary, the treaty shall prevail, and such party shall be allowed to withdraw from the operations against that state."

Spain had just concluded a treaty with Algiers at the expense of 3. millions of dollars, and did not like to relinquish the benefit of that until the other party should fail in their observance of it. Portugal, Naples, the two Sicilies, Venice, Malta, Denmark and Sweden were favorably disposed to such an association; but their representatives at Paris expressed apprehensions that France would interfere, and, either openly or secretly support the Barbary powers; and they required that I should ascertain the dispositions of the Count de Vergennes on the subject. I had before taken occasion to inform him of what we were proposing, and therefore did not think it proper to insinuate any doubt of the fair conduct of his government; but stating our propositions, I mentioned the apprehensions entertained by us that England would interfere in behalf of those piratical governments. " She dares not do it," said he. I pressed it no further. The other agents were

satisfied with this indication of his sentiments, and
nothing was now wanting to bring it into direct and
formal consideration, but the assent of our government, and their authority to make the formal proposition. I communicated to them the favorable
prospect of protecting our commerce from the Barbary depredations, and for such a continuance of
time as, by an exclusion of them from the sea, to
change their habits & characters from a predatory to
an agricultural people: towards which however it
was expected they would contribute a frigate, and
it's expenses to be in constant cruise. But they
were in no condition to make any such engagement.
Their recommendatory powers for obtaining contributions were so openly neglected by the several
states that they declined an engagement which they
were conscious they could not fulfill with punctuality;
and so it fell through.

May 17. In 1786. while at Paris I became acquainted with John Ledyard of Connecticut, a man
of genius, of some science, and of fearless courage, &
enterprise. He had accompanied Capt Cook in his
voyage to the Pacific, had distinguished himself on
several occasions by an unrivalled intrepidity, and
published an account of that voyage with details un-
favorable to Cook's deportment towards the savages,
and lessening our regrets at his fate. Ledyard had
come to Paris in the hope of forming a company to
engage in the fur trade of the Western coast of
America. He was disappointed in this, and being
out of business, and of a roaming, restless character,
I suggested to him the enterprise of exploring the

Western part of our continent, by passing thro St.
Petersburg to Kamschatka, and procuring a passage
thence in some of the Russian vessels to Nootka
Sound, whence he might make his way across the
continent to America; and I undertook to have the
permission of the Empress of Russia solicited. He
eagerly embraced the proposition, and M. de Sémou-
lin, the Russian Ambassador, and more particularly
Baron Grimm the special correspondent of the Empress, solicited her permission for him to pass thro'
her dominions to the Western coast of America.
And here I must correct a material error which I
have committed in another place to the prejudice of
the Empress. In writing some Notes of the life of
Capt Lewis,[1] prefixed to his expedition to the Pacific,
I stated that the Empress gave the permission asked,
& afterwards retracted it. This idea, after a lapse
of 26 years, had so insinuated itself into my mind,
that I committed it to paper without the least suspi-
cion of error. Yet I find, on recurring to my letters
of that date that the Empress refused permission at
once, considering the enterprise as entirely chimeri-
cal. But Ledyard would not relinquish it, persuad-
ing himself that by proceeding to St. Petersburg
he could satisfy the Empress of it's practicability and obtain her permission. He went accordingly, but she was absent on a visit to some distant
part of her dominions,[2] and he pursued his course
to within 200. miles of Kamschatka, where he was
overtaken by an arrest from the Empress, brought
back to Poland, and there dismissed. I must there-

---

[1] In Lewis and Clarke's *Travels*.   [2] The Crimea.—*T. J.*

fore in justice, acquit the Empress of ever having
for a moment countenanced, even by the indulgence
of an innocent passage thro' her territories this interesting enterprise.

May 18. The pecuniary distresses of France produced this year a measure of which there had been
no example for near two centuries, & the consequences of which, good and evil, are not yet calcula-
ble. For it's remote causes we must go a little back.

Celebrated writers of France and England had
already sketched good principles on the subject of
government. Yet the American Revolution seems
first to have awakened the thinking part of the
French nation in general from the sleep of despotism
in which they were sunk. The officers too who had
been to America, were mostly young men, less
shackled by habit and prejudice, and more ready to
assent to the suggestions of common sense, and feel-
ing of common rights. They came back with new
ideas & impressions. The press, notwithstanding
it's shackles, began to disseminate them. Conversation assumed new freedoms. Politics became the
theme of all societies, male and female, and a very
extensive & zealous party was formed which acquired the appellation of the Patriotic party, who,
sensible of the abusive government under which
they lived, sighed for occasions of reforming it.
This party comprehended all the honesty of the
kingdom sufficiently at it's leisure to think, the men
of letters, the easy Bourgeois, the young nobility
partly from reflection, partly from mode, for these
sentiments became matter of mode, and as such

united most of the young women to the party.
Happily for the nation, it happened at the same
moment that the dissipations of the Queen and
court, the abuses of the pension-list, and dilapida-
tions in the administration of every branch of the
finances, had exhausted the treasures and credit
of the nation, insomuch that it's most necessary
functions were paralyzed. To reform these abuses
would have overset the minister; to impose new
taxes by the authority of the King was known to be
impossible from the determined opposition of the
parliament to their enregistry. No resource remained then but to appeal to the nation. He advised therefore the call of an assembly of the most
distinguished characters of the nation, in the hope
that by promises of various and valuable improvements in the organization and regimen of the government, they would be induced to authorize new taxes,
to controul the opposition of the parliament, and to
raise the annual revenue to the level of expenditures.
An Assembly of Notables therefore, about 150. in
number named by the King, convened on the 22d.
of Feb. The Minister (Calonne) stated to them
that the annual excess of expenses beyond the
revenue, when Louis XVI. came to the throne, was
37. millions of livres; that 440. millns. had been
borrowed to reestablish the navy; that the American
war had cost them 1440. millns. (256. mils. of Dollars)
and that the interest of these sums, with other increased expenses had added 40 millns. more to the
annual deficit. (But a subseqt. and more candid
estimate made it 56. millns.) He proffered them an

universal redress of grievances, laid open those grievances fully, pointed out sound remedies, and covering his canvas with objects of this magnitude, the
deficit dwindled to a little accessory, scarcely attracting attention. The persons chosen were the
most able & independent characters in the kingdom,
and their support, if it could be obtained, would be
enough for him. They improved the occasion for
redressing their grievances, and agreed that the
public wants should be relieved; but went into an
examination of the causes of them. It was supposed that Calonne was conscious that his accounts
could not bear examination; and it was said and
believed that he asked of the King to send 4. members to the Bastile, of whom the M. de la Fayette was
one, to banish 20. others, & 2. of his Ministers. The
King found it shorter to banish him. His successor
went on in full concert with the Assembly. The
result was an augmentation of the revenue a promise of economies in it's expenditure, of an annual
settlement of the public accounts before a council,
which the Comptroller, having been heretofore
obliged to settle only with the King in person, of
course never settled at all; an acknowledgment that
the King could not lay a new tax, a reformation of
the criminal laws abolition of torture, suppression
of Corvées, reformation of the gabelles, removal of
the interior custom houses, free commerce of grain
internal & external, and the establishment of Provincial assemblies; which alltogether constituted a
great mass of improvement in the condition of the
nation. The establishment of the Provincial assem-

blies was in itself a fundamental improvement. They would be of the choice of the people, one third renewed every year, in those provinces where there are no States, that is to say over about three fourths of the kingdom. They would be partly an Executive themselves, & partly an Executive council to the Intendant, to whom the Executive power, in his province had been heretofore entirely delegated. Chosen by the people, they would soften the execution of hard laws, & having a right of representation to the King, they would censure bad laws, suggest good ones, expose abuses, and their representations, when united, would command respect. To the other advantages might be added the precedent itself of calling the Assemblée des Notables, which would perhaps grow into habit. The hope was that the improvements thus promised would be carried into effect, that they would be maintained during the present reign, & that that would be long enough for them to take some root in the constitution, so that they might come to be considered as a part of that, and be protected by time, and the attachment of the nation.

The Count de Vergennes had died a few days before the meeting of the Assembly, & the Count de Montmorin had been named Minister of foreign affairs in his place. Villedeuil succeeded Calonnes as Comptroller general, & Lomenie de Bryenne, Archbishop of Thoulouse, afterwards of Sens, & ultimately Cardinal Lomenie, was named Minister principal, with whom the other ministers were to transact the business of their departments, hereto-

fore done with the King in person, and the Duke de
Nivernois, and M. de Malesherbes were called to the
Council.   On the nomination of the Minister principal the Marshals de Segur & de Castries retired from
the departments of War & Marine, unwilling to act
subordinately, or to share the blame of proceedings
taken out of their direction.   They were succeeded
by the Count de Brienne, brother of the Prime
minister, and the Marquis de la Luzerne, brother to
him who had been Minister in the United States.

May 24.   A dislocated wrist, unsuccessfully set,
occasioned advice from my Surgeon to try the min-
eral waters of Aix in Provence as a corroborant.   I
left Paris for that place therefore on the 28th. of
Feb. and proceeded up the Seine, thro' Champagne
& Burgundy, and down the Rhone thro' the Beau-
jolais by Lyons, Avignon, Nismes to Aix, where
finding on trial no benefit from the waters, I concluded to visit the rice country of Piedmont, to see
if anything might be learned there to benefit the
rivalship of our Carolina rice with that, and thence
to make a tour of the seaport towns of France, along
it's Southern and Western Coast, to inform myself
if anything could be done to favor our commerce
with them.[1]   From Aix therefore I took my route by
Marseilles, Toulon, Hieres, Nice, across the Col de
Tende, by Coni, Turin, Vercelli, Novara, Milan,
Pavia, Novi, Genoa.   Thence returning along the
coast by Savona, Noli, Albenga, Oneglia, Monaco,
Nice, Antibes, Frejus, Aix, Marseilles, Avignon,

---

[1] In Washington's edition of Jefferson's Writings (ix., 313) a journal
of this tour is printed.

Nismes, Montpellier, Frontignan, Cette, Agde, and along the canal of Languedoc, by Bezieres, Narbonne, Cascassonne, Castelnaudari, thro' the Souterrain of St. Feriol and back by Castelnaudari, to Toulouse, thence to Montauban & down the Garonne by Langon to Bordeaux. Thence to Rochefort, la Rochelle, Nantes, L'Orient, then back by Rennes to Nantes, and up the Loire by Angers, Tours, Amboise, Blois to New Orleans, thence direct to Paris where I arrived on the 10th. of June. Soon after my return from this journey to wit, about the latter part of July, I received my younger daughter Maria from Virginia by the way of London, the youngest having died some time before.

The treasonable perfidy of the Prince of Orange, Stadtholder & Captain General of the United Netherlands, in the war which England waged against them for entering into a treaty of commerce with the U. S. is known to all. As their Executive officer, charged with the conduct of the war, he contrived to baffle all the measures of the States General, to dislocate all their military plans, & played false into the hands of England and against his own country on every possible occasion, confident in her protection, and in that of the King of Prussia, brother to his Princess. The States General indignant at this patricidal conduct applied to France for aid, according to the stipulations of the treaty concluded with her in 85. It was assured to them readily, and in cordial terms, in a letter from the Ct. de Vergennes to the Marquis de Verac, Ambassador of France at the Hague, of which the following is an extract.

"Extrait de la depeche de Monsr. le Comte de Vergennes à Monsr. le Marquis de Verac, Ambassadeur de France à la Haye, du 1er Mars 1786.

"Le Roi concourrera, autant qu'il sera en son pouvoir, au succes de la chose, et vous inviterez de sa part les patriotes de lui communiquer leurs vues, leurs plans, et leurs envieux. Vous les assurerez que le roi prend un interêt veritable à leurs personnes comme à leur cause, et qu'ils peuvent compter sur sa protection. Ils doivent y compter d'autant plus, Monsieur, que nous ne dissimulons pas que si Monsr. le Stadhoulder reprend son ancienne influence, le systeme Anglois ne tardera pas de prevaloir, et que notre alliance deviendroit un être de raison. Les Patriotes sentiront facilement que cette position seroit incompatible avec la dignité, comme avec la consideration de sa majesté. Mais dans le cas. Monsieur, ou les chefs des Patriotes auroient à craindre une scission, ils auroient le temps suffisant pour ramener ceux de leurs amis que les Anglomanes ont egarés, et preparer les choses de maniere que la question de nouveau mise en deliberation soit decidé selon leurs desirs. Dans cette hypothese, le roi vous autorise à agir de concert avec eux, de suivre la direction qu'ils jugeront devoir vous donner, et d'employer tous les moyens pour augmenter le nombre des partisans de la bonne cause. Il me reste, Monsieur, il me reste, Monsieur, de vous parler de la sureté personelle des patriotes. Vous les assurerez que dans tout etat de cause, le roi les prend sous sa protection immediate, et vous ferez connoitre partout ou vous le jugerez necessaire, que sa Majesté

regarderoit comme une offense personnelle tout ce
qu' on entreprenderoit contre leur liberte.   Il est à
presumer que ce langage, tenu avec energie, en
imposera à l'audace des Anglomanes et que Monsr.
le Prince de Nassau croira courir quelque risque en
provoquant le ressentiment de sa Majesté."

This letter was communicated by the Patriots
to me when at Amsterdam in 1788. and a copy
sent by me to Mr. Jay in my letter to him of Mar.
16. 1788.

The object of the Patriots was to establish a representative and republican government.   The majority of the States general were with them, but the
majority of the populace of the towns was with the
Prince of Orange; and that populace was played off
with great effect by the triumvirate of * * *
Harris [1] the English Ambassador afterwards Ld.
Malmesbury, the Prince of Orange a stupid man, and
the Princess as much a man as either of her colleagues
in audaciousness, in enterprise, & in the thirst of
domination.   By these the mobs of the Hague were
excited against the members of the States general,
their persons were insulted & endangered in the
streets, the sanctuary of their houses was violated,
and the Prince whose function & duty it was to re-
press and punish these violations of order, took no
steps for that purpose.   The States General, for
their own protection were therefore obliged to place
their militia under the command of a Committee.
The Prince filled the courts of London and Berlin

[1] Sir James Harris.

with complaints at this usurpation of his prerogatives, and forgetting that he was but the first servant
of a republic, marched his regular troops against the
city of Utrecht, where the States were in session.
They were repulsed by the militia. His interests
now became marshalled with those of the public
enemy & against his own country. The States
therefore, exercising their rights of sovereignty, deprived him of all his powers. The great Frederic
had died in August 86.[1] He had never intended to
break with France in support of the Prince of Orange.
During the illness of which he died, he had thro' the
Duke of Brunswick, declared to the Marquis de la
Fayette, who was then at Berlin, that he meant not
to support the English interest in Holland: that he
might assure the government of France his only wish
was that some honorable place in the Constitution
should be reserved for the Stadtholder and his children, and that he would take no part in the quarrel
unless an entire abolition of the Stadtholderate
should be attempted. But his place was now occupied by Frederic William, his great nephew, a man
of little understanding, much caprice, & very in-
considerate; and the Princess his sister, altho' her
husband was in arms against the legitimate authorities of the country, attempting to go to Amsterdam for the purpose of exciting the mobs of that
place and being refused permission to pass a military
post on the way, he put the Duke of Brunswick at
the head of 20,000 men, and made demonstrations of
marching on Holland. The King of France hereupon

[1] lre to Jay Aug. 6. 87.—*T. J.*

declared, by his Chargé des Affaires in Holland that if the Prussian troops continued to menace Holland with an invasion, his Majesty, in quality of Ally, was determined to succor that province.[1]   In answer to this Eden gave official information to Count Montmorin, that England must consider as at an end, it's convention with France relative to giving notice of it's naval armaments and that she was arming generally.[2]   War being now imminent, Eden questioned me on the effect of our treaty with France in the case of a war, & what might be our dispositions.   I told him frankly and without hesitation that our dispositions would be neutral, and that I thought it would be the interest of both these powers that we should be so; because it would relieve both from all anxiety as to feeding their W. India islands.   That England too, by suffering us to remain so, would avoid a heavy land-war on our continent, which might very much cripple her proceedings elsewhere; that our treaty indeed obliged us to receive into our ports the armed vessels of France, with their prizes, and to refuse admission to the prizes made on her by her enemies: that there was a clause also by which we guaranteed to France her American possessions, which might perhaps force us into the war, if these were attacked.   "Then it will be war, said he, for they will assuredly be attacked."[3]   Liston, at Madrid, about the same time, made the same inquiries of Carmichael.   The government of France then declared a determination to

[1] My lre Sep. 22. 87.—*T. J.*   [2] My lre to J. Jay Sep. 24.—*T. J.*
[3] lre to Carm. Dec. 15.—*T. J.*

form a camp of observation at Givet, commenced arming her marine, and named the Bailli de Suffrein their Generalissimo on the Ocean. She secretly engaged also in negotiations with Russia, Austria, & Spain to form a quadruple alliance. The Duke of Brunswick having advanced to the confines of Holland, sent some of his officers to Givet to reconnoitre the state of things there, and report them to him. He said afterwards that "if there had been only a few tents at that place, he should not have advanced further, for that the King would not merely for the interest of his sister, engage in a war with France." But finding that there was not a single company there, he boldly entered the country took their towns as fast as he presented himself before them, and advanced on Utrecht. The States had appointed the Rhingrave of Salm their Commander-in-chief, a Prince without talents, without courage, and without principle. He might have held out in Utrecht for a considerable time, but he surrendered the place without firing a gun, literally ran away & hid himself so that for months it was not known what had become of him. Amsterdam was then attacked and capitulated. In the meantime the negotiations for the quadruple alliance were proceeding favorably. But the secrecy with which they were attempted to be conducted, was penetrated by Fraser, Chargé des affaires of England at St. Petersburg, who instantly notified his court, and gave the alarm to Prussia. The King saw at once what would be his situation between the jaws of France, Austria, and Russia. In great dismay he besought the court of London not to abandon him, sent Alvensleben to Paris to explain and soothe, and England thro' the D. of Dorset and Eden, renewed her conferences for accommodation. The Archbishop, who shuddered at the idea of war, and preferred a peaceful surrender of right to an armed vindication of it, received them with open arms, entered into cordial conferences, and a declaration, and counter declaration were cooked up at Versailles and sent to London for approbation. They were approved there, reached Paris at 1 o'clock of the 27th. and were signed that night at Versailles. It was said and believed at Paris that M. de Montmorin, literally " pleuroit comme un enfant," when obliged to sign this counter declaration; so distressed was he by the dishonor of sacrificing the Patriots after assurances so solemn of protection, and absolute encouragement to proceed.[1] The Prince of Orange was reinstated in all his powers, now become regal. A great emigration of the Patriots took place, all were deprived of office, many exiled, and their property confiscated. They were received in France, and subsisted for some time on her bounty. Thus fell Holland, by the treachery of her chief, from her honorable independence to become a province of England, and so also her Stadtholder from the high station of the first citizen of a free republic, to be the servile Viceroy of a foreign sovereign. And this was effected by a mere scene of bullying & demonstration, not one of the parties, France England or Prussia having ever really meant to encounter actual war

[1] My lre to Jay Nov. 3. lre to J. Adams, Nov. 13.—*T. J.*

for the interest of the Prince of Orange.   But it had all the effect of a real and decisive war.

Our first essay in America to establish a federative government had fallen, on trial, very short of it's object.   During the war of Independance, while the pressure of an external enemy hooped us together, and their enterprises kept us necessarily on the alert, the spirit of the people, excited by danger, was a supplement to the Confederation, and urged them to zealous exertions, whether claimed by that instrument, or not.   But when peace and safety were restored, and every man became engaged in useful and profitable occupation, less attention was paid to the calls of Congress.   The fundamental defect of the Confederation was that Congress was not authorized to act immediately on the people, & by it's own officers.   Their power was only requisitory, and these requisitions were addressed to the several legislatures, to be by them carried into execution, without other coercion than the moral principle of duty.   This allowed in fact a negative to every legislature, on every measure proposed by Congress; a negative so frequently exercised in practice as to benumb the action of the federal government, and to render it inefficient in it's general objects, & more especially in pecuniary and foreign concerns.   The want too of a separation of the legislative, executive, & judiciary functions worked disadvantageously in practice.   Yet this state of things afforded a happy augury of the future march of our confederacy, when it was seen that the good sense and good dispositions of the people, as soon as they perceived the incompetence of their first compact, instead of leaving it's correction to insurrection and civil war, agreed with one voice to elect deputies to a general convention, who should peaceably meet and agree on such a constitution as "would ensure peace, justice, liberty, the common defence & general welfare."

This Convention met at Philadelphia on the 25th. of May '87. It sate with closed doors, and kept all it's proceedings secret, until it's dissolution on the 17th. of September, when the results of their labors were published all together. I received a copy early in November, and read and contemplated it's provisions with great satisfaction. As not a member of the Convention however, nor probably a single citizen of the Union, had approved it in all it's parts, so I too found articles which I thought objectionable. The absence of express declarations ensuring freedom of religion, freedom of the press, freedom of the person under the uninterrupted protection of the Habeas corpus, & trial by jury in civil as well as in criminal cases excited my jealousy; and the re-eligibility of the President for life, I quite disapproved. I expressed freely in letters to my friends, and most particularly to Mr. Madison & General Washington, my approbations and objections. How the good should be secured, and the ill brought to rights was the difficulty. To refer it back to a new Convention might endanger the loss of the whole. My first idea was that the 9. states first acting should accept it unconditionally, and thus secure what in it was good, and that the 4. last should accept on the previous condition that

certain amendments should be agreed to, but a better course was devised of accepting the whole and
trusting that the good sense & honest intention
of our citizens would make the alterations which
should be deemed necessary. Accordingly all accepted, 6. without objection, and 7. with recom-
mendations of specified amendments. Those respecting the press, religion, & juries, with several
others, of great value, were accordingly made; but
the Habeas corpus was left to the discretion of Congress, and the amendment against the reeligibility
of the President was not proposed by that body.
My fears of that feature were founded on the importance of the office, on the fierce contentions it
might excite among ourselves, if continuable for
life, and the dangers of interference either with
money or arms, by foreign nations, to whom the
choice of an American President might become interesting. Examples of this abounded in history; in
the case of the Roman emperors for instance, of the
Popes while of any significance, of the German emperors, the Kings of Poland, & the Deys of Barbary.
I had observed too in the feudal History, and in the
recent instance particularly of the Stadtholder of
Holland, how easily offices or tenures for life slide
into inheritances. My wish therefore was that the
President should be elected for 7. years & be ineligible afterwards. This term I thought sufficient to
enable him, with the concurrence of the legislature,
to carry thro' & establish any system of improvement he should propose for the general good. But
the practice adopted I think is better allowing his

continuance for 8. years with a liability to be dropped at half way of the term, making that a period of probation. That his continuance should be restrained to 7. years was the opinion of the Convention at an early stage of it's session, when it voted that term by a majority of 8. against 2. and by a simple majority that he should be ineligible a second time. This opinion &c. was confirmed by the house so late as July 26, referred to the committee of detail, rereported favorably by them, and changed to the present form by final vote on the last day but one only of their session.[1] Of this change three states expressed their disapprobation, N. York by recommending an amendment that the President should not be eligible a third time, and Virginia and N. Carolina that he should not be capable of serving more than 8. in any term of 16. years. And altho' this amendment has not been made in form, yet practice seems to have established it. The example of 4 Presidents voluntarily retiring at the end of their 8th year, & the progress of public opinion that the principle is salutary, have given it in practice the force of precedent & usage; insomuch that should a President consent to be a candidate for a 3d. election, I trust he would be rejected on this demonstration of ambitious views.

But there was another amendment of which none of us thought at the time and in the omission of which lurks the germ that is to destroy this happy

[1] This is an evident error. On September 4th, the committee of eleven reported a clause making the term four years, which was adopted by the convention on the 6th, and not altered thereafter.

combination of National powers in the General government for matters of National concern, and independent powers in the states for what concerns the
states severally.   In England it was a great point
gained at the Revolution, that the commissions of
the judges, which had hitherto been during pleasure,
should thenceforth be made during good behavior.
A Judiciary dependent on the will of the King had
proved itself the most oppressive of all tools in the
hands of that Magistrate.   Nothing then could be
more salutary than a change there to the tenure of
good behavior; and the question of good behavior
left to the vote of a simple majority in the two houses
of parliament.   Before the revolution we were all
good English Whigs, cordial in their free principles,
and in their jealousies of their executive Magistrate.
These jealousies are very apparent in all our state
constitutions; and, in the general government in
this instance, we have gone even beyond the English
caution, by requiring a vote of two thirds in one of
the Houses for removing a judge; a vote so impossible where [1] any defence is made, before men of
ordinary prejudices & passions, that our judges are
effectually independent of the nation.   But this
ought not to be.   I would not indeed make them
dependant on the Executive authority, as they
formerly were in England; but I deem it indispensable to the continuance of this government
that they should be submitted to some practical &

---

[1] In the impeachment of judge Pickering of New Hampshire, a
habitual & maniac drunkard, no defence was made.   Had there been,
the party vote of more than one third of the Senate would have acquitted him.—*T. J.*

impartial controul: and that this, to be imparted, must be compounded of a mixture of state and federal authorities.   It is not enough that honest men are appointed judges.   All know the influence of interest on the mind of man, and how unconsciously his judgment is warped by that influence.   To this bias add that of the esprit de corps, of their peculiar maxim and creed that "it is the office of a good judge to enlarge his jurisdiction," and the absence of responsibility, and how can we expect impartial decision between the General government, of which they are themselves so eminent a part, and an individual state from which they have nothing to hope or fear.   We have seen too that, contrary to all correct example, they are in the habit of going out of the question before them, to throw an anchor ahead and grapple further hold for future advances of power.   They are then in fact the corps of sappers & miners, steadily working to undermine the independant rights of the States, & to consolidate all power in the hands of that government in which they have so important a freehold estate.   But it is not by the consolidation, or concentration of powers, but by their distribution, that good government is effected.   Were not this great country already divided into states, that division must be made, that each might do for itself what concerns itself directly, and what it can so much better do than a distant authority.   Every state again is divided into counties, each to take care of what lies within it's local bounds; each county again into townships or wards, to manage minuter details; and every ward into

farms, to be governed each by it's individual pro-
prietor. Were we directed from Washington when
to sow, & when to reap, we should soon want bread.
It is by this partition of cares, descending in gradation from general to particular, that the mass of
human affairs may be best managed for the good
and prosperity of all. I repeat that I do not charge
the judges with wilful and ill-intentioned error; but
honest error must be arrested where it's toleration
leads to public ruin. As, for the safety of society,
we commit honest maniacs to Bedlam, so judges
should be withdrawn from their bench, whose erroneous biases are leading us to dissolution. It may indeed injure them in fame or in fortune; but it saves
the republic, which is the first and supreme law.

Among the debilities of the government of the
Confederation, no one was more distinguished or
more distressing than the utter impossibility of obtaining, from the states, the monies necessary for
the payment of debts, or even for the ordinary expenses of the government. Some contributed a
little, some less, & some nothing, and the last furnished at length an excuse for the first to do nothing
also. Mr. Adams, while residing at the Hague, had
a general authority to borrow what sums might be
requisite for ordinary & necessary expenses. Interest on the public debt, and the maintenance of
the diplomatic establishment in Europe, had been
habitually provided in this way. He was now
elected Vice President of the U S. was soon to return
to America,[1] and had referred our bankers to me for

---

[1] Adams returned to America before his election as Vice President.

future councel on our affairs in their hands. But I
had no powers, no instructions, no means, and no
familiarity with the subject. It had always been
exclusively under his management, except as to
occasional and partial deposits in the hands of Mr.
Grand, banker in Paris, for special and local purposes. These last had been exhausted for some
time, and I had fervently pressed the Treasury board
to replenish this particular deposit; as Mr. Grand
now refused to make further advances. They answered candidly that no funds could be obtained
until the new government should get into action, and
have time to make it's arrangements. Mr. Adams
had received his appointment to the court of London
while engaged at Paris, with Dr. Franklin and myself, in the negotiations under our joint commissions.
He had repaired thence to London, without returning to the Hague to take leave of that government.
He thought it necessary however to do so now, before he should leave Europe, and accordingly went
there. I learned his departure from London by a
letter from Mrs. Adams received on the very day on
which he would arrive at the Hague. A consultation
with him, & some provision for the future was indispensable, while we could yet avail ourselves of his
powers. For when they would be gone, we should
be without resource. I was daily dunned by a company who had formerly made a small loan to the U
S. the principal of which was now become due; and
our bankers in Amsterdam had notified me that the
interest on our general debt would be expected in
June; that if we failed to pay it, it would be deemed

an act of bankruptcy and would effectually destroy
the credit of the U. S. and all future prospect of obtaining money there; that the loan they had been
authorized to open, of which a third only was filled,
had now ceased to get forward, and rendered desperate that hope of resource. I saw that there was
not a moment to lose, and set out for the Hague on
the 2d. morning after receiving the information of
Mr. Adams's journey. I went the direct road by
Louvres, Senlis, Roye, Pont St. Maxence, Bois le
duc, Gournay, Peronne, Cambray, Bouchain, Valen-
ciennes, Mons, Bruxelles, Malines, Antwerp, Mor-
dick, and Rotterdam, to the Hague, where I happily
found Mr. Adams. He concurred with me at once
in opinion that something must be done, and that we
ought to risk ourselves on doing it without instructions, to save the credit of the U S. We foresaw
that before the new government could be adopted,
assembled, establish it's financial system, get the
money into the treasury, and place it in Europe,
considerable time would elapse; that therefore we
had better provide at once for the years 88. 89. & 90.
in order to place our government at it's ease, and
our credit in security, during that trying interval.
We set out therefore by the way of Leyden for Amsterdam, where we arrived on the 10th. I had prepared an estimate showing that

	Florins.
there would be necessary for the year 88—	531,937–10
89—	538,540
90—	473,540
Total,	1,544,017–10

	Flor.	
to meet this the bankers had in hand	79,268–2–8	
& the unsold bonds would yield	542,800	622,068–2–8
leaving a deficit of		921,949–7–4
we proposed then to borrow a million yielding .		920,000
which would leave a small deficiency of .		1,949–7–4

Mr. Adams accordingly executed 1000. bonds, for 1000. florins each, and deposited them in the hands of our bankers, with instructions however not to issue them until Congress should ratify the measure. This done, he returned to London, and I set out for Paris; and as nothing urgent forbade it, I determined to return along the banks of the Rhine to Strasburg, and thence strike off to Paris. I accordingly left Amsterdam on the 30th of March, and proceeded by Utrecht, Nimeguen, Cleves, Duysberg, Dusseldorf, Cologne, Bonne, Coblentz, Nassau, Hocheim, Frankfort, & made an excursion to Hanau, thence to Mayence and another excursion to Rudesheim, & Johansberg; then by Oppenheim, Worms, and Manheim, and an excursion to Heidelberg, then by Spire, Carlsruh, Rastadt & Kelh, to Strasburg, where I arrived Apr. 16th, and proceeded again on the 18th, by Phalsbourg, Fenestrange, Dieuze, Moyenvie, Nancy, Toul, Ligny, Barleduc, St. Diziers, Vitry, Chalons sur Marne, Epernay, Chateau Thierri, Meaux, to Paris where I arrived on the 23d. of April [1]; and I had the satisfaction to reflect that by this journey our credit was secured, the new government was placed at ease for two years to come, and that

[1] A journal of this tour, kept by Jefferson, is printed in Washington's edition of his writings, ix., 373.

as well as myself were relieved from the torment of incessant duns, whose just complaints could not be silenced by any means within our power.

A Consular Convention had been agreed on in 84. between Dr. Franklin and the French government containing several articles so entirely inconsistent with the laws of the several states, and the general spirit of our citizens, that Congress withheld their ratification, and sent it back to me with instructions to get those articles expunged or modified so as to render them compatible with our laws. The minister retired unwillingly from these concessions, which indeed authorized the exercise of powers very offensive in a free state. After much discussion it was reformed in a considerable degree, and the Convention was signed by the Count Montmorin and myself, on the 14th. of Nov. 88 not indeed such as I would have wished; but such as could be obtained with good humor & friendship.[1]

On my return from Holland, I had found Paris still in high fermentation as I had left it. Had the Archbishop, on the close of the assembly of Notables, immediately carried into operation the measures contemplated, it was believed they would all have been registered by the parliament, but he was slow, presented his edicts, one after another, & at considerable intervals of time, which gave time for the feelings excited by the proceedings of the Notables to cool off, new claims to be advanced, and a pressure

[1] Among the Jefferson MSS. in the Department of State are printed copies of both the consular conventions negotiated by Franklin and Jefferson, and the original draft of the latter, in Jefferson's handwriting.

to arise for a fixed constitution, not subject to changes at the will of the King. Nor should we wonder at this pressure when we consider the monstrous abuses of power under which this people were ground to powder, when we pass in review the weight of their taxes, and inequality of their distribution; the oppressions of the tythes, of the tailles, the corvées, the gabelles, the farms & barriers; the shackles on Commerce by monopolies; on Industry by gilds & corporations; on the freedom of conscience, of thought, and of speech; on the Press by the Censure; and of person by lettres de Cachet. the cruelty of the criminal code generally, the atrocities of the Rack, the venality of judges, and their partialities to the rich; the Monopoly of Military honors by the Noblesse; the enormous expenses of the Queen, the princes & the Court; the prodigalities of pensions; & the riches, luxury, indolence & immorality of the clergy. Surely under such a mass of misrule and oppression, a people might justly press for a thoro' reformation, and might even dismount their rough-shod riders, & leave them to walk on their own legs. The edicts relative to the corvées & free circulation of grain, were first presented to the parliament and registered. But those for the impôt territorial, & stamp tax, offered some time after, were refused by the parliament, which proposed a call of the States General as alone competent to their authorization. Their refusal produced a Bed of justice, and their exile to Troyes. The advocates however refusing to attend them, a suspension in the administration of justice took place.

The Parliament held out for awhile, but the ennui of their exile and absence from Paris begun at length to be felt, and some dispositions for compromise to appear. On their consent therefore to prolong some of the former taxes, they were recalled from exile, the King met them in session Nov. 19. 87. promised to call the States General in the year 92. and a majority expressed their assent to register an edict for successive and annual loans from 1788. to 92. But a protest being entered by the Duke of Orleans and this encouraging others in a disposition to retract, the King ordered peremptorily the registry of the edict, and left the assembly abruptly. The parliament immediately protested that the votes for the enregistry had not been legally taken, and that they gave no sanction to the loans proposed. This was enough to discredit and defeat them. Hereupon issued another edict for the establishment of a cour plenière, and the suspension of all the parliaments in the kingdom. This being opposed as might be expected by reclamations from all the parliaments & provinces, the King gave way and by an edict of July 5. 88 renounced his cour plenière, & promised the States General for the 1st. of May of the ensuing year: and the Archbishop finding the times beyond his faculties, accepted the promise of a Cardinal's hat, was removed [Sep. 88] from the ministry, and Mr. Necker was called to the department of finance. The innocent rejoicings of the people of Paris on this change provoked the interference of an officer of the city guards, whose order for their dispersion not being obeyed, he charged them with fixed bayonets, killed two or three, and wounded many. This dispersed them for the moment; but they collected the next day in great numbers, burnt 10. or 12. guard houses, killed two or three of the guards, & lost 6. or 8. more of their own number. The city was hereupon put under martial law, and after awhile the tumult subsided. The effect of this change of ministers, and the promise of the States General at an early day, tranquillized the nation. But two great questions now occurred. 1. What proportion shall the number of deputies of the tiers etat bear to those of the Nobles and Clergy? And 2. shall they sit in the same, or in distinct apartments? Mr. Necker, desirous of avoiding himself these knotty questions, proposed a second call of the same Notables, and that their advice should be asked on the subject. They met Nov. 9. 88. and, by five bureaux against one, they recommended the forms of the States General of 1614. wherein the houses were separate, and voted by orders, not by persons. But the whole nation declaring at once against this, and that the tiers etat should be, in numbers, equal to both the other orders, and the Parliament deciding for the same proportion, it was determined so to be, by a declaration of Dec. 27. 88. A Report of Mr. Necker to the King, of about the same date, contained other very important concessions. 1. That the King could neither lay a new tax, nor prolong an old one. 2. It expressed a readiness to agree on the periodical meeting of the States. 3. To consult on the necessary restriction on lettres de Cachet. And 4. how far the Press might be made free. 5. It admits that

the States are to appropriate the public money; and
6. that Ministers shall be responsible for public expenditures. And these concessions came from the
very heart of the King. He had not a wish but for
the good of the nation, and for that object no personal sacrifice would ever have cost him a moment's
regret. But his mind was weakness itself, his constitution timid, his judgment null, and without
sufficient firmness even to stand by the faith of his
word. His Queen too, haughty and bearing no
contradiction, had an absolute ascendency over him;
and around her were rallied the King's brother d'Artois, the court generally, and the aristocratic part of
his ministers, particularly Breteuil, Broglio, Vauguyon, Foulon, Luzerne, men whose principles of
government were those of the age of Louis XIV.
Against this host the good counsels of Necker, Montmorin, St. Priest, altho' in unison with the wishes of
the King himself, were of little avail. The resolutions of the morning formed under their advice,
would be reversed in the evening by the influence of
the Queen & court. But the hand of heaven weighed
heavily indeed on the machinations of this junto;
producing collateral incidents, not arising out of the
case, yet powerfully co-exciting the nation to force
a regeneration of it's government, and overwhelming
with accumulated difficulties this liberticide resistance. For, while laboring under the want of money
for even ordinary purposes, in a government which
required a million of livres a day, and driven to the
last ditch by the universal call for liberty, there
came on a winter of such severe cold, as was without

example in the memory of man, or in the written
records of history.   The Mercury was at times 50°
below the freezing point of Fahrenheit and 22° below
that of Reaumur.   All out-door labor was suspended,
and the poor, without the wages of labor, were of
course without either bread or fuel.   The government found it's necessities aggravated by that of
procuring immense quantities of fire-wood, and of
keeping great fires at all the cross-streets, around
which the people gathered in crowds to avoid perish-
ing with cold.   Bread too was to be bought, and
distributed daily gratis, until a relaxation of the
season should enable the people to work: and the
slender stock of bread-stuff had for some time threatened famine, and had raised that article to an enormous price.   So great indeed was the scarcity of
bread that from the highest to the lowest citizen,
the bakers were permitted to deal but a scanty
allowance per head, even to those who paid for it;
and in cards of invitation to dine in the richest
houses, the guest was notified to bring his own bread.
To eke out the existence of the people, every person
who had the means, was called on for a weekly sub-
scription, which the Curés collected and employed
in providing messes for the nourishment of the poor,
and vied with each other in devising such economical
compositions of food as would subsist the greatest
number with the smallest means.   This want of
bread had been foreseen for some time past and M.
de Montmorin had desired me to notify it in America,
and that, in addition to the market price, a premium
should be given on what should be brought from

the U S. Notice was accordingly given and produced considerable supplies. Subsequent information
made the importations from America, during the
months of March, April & May, into the Atlantic
ports of France, amount to about 21,000 barrels of
flour, besides what went to other ports, and in other
months, while our supplies to their West-Indian
islands relieved them also from that drain. This
distress for bread continued till July.

Hitherto no acts of popular violence had been produced by the struggle for political reformation.
Little riots, on ordinary incidents, had taken place,
as at other times, in different parts of the kingdom,
in which some lives, perhaps a dozen or twenty, had
been lost, but in the month of April a more serious
one occurred in Paris, unconnected indeed with the
revolutionary principle, but making part of the history of the day. The Fauxbourg St. Antoine is a
quarter of the city inhabited entirely by the class of
day-laborers and journeymen in every line. A ru-
mor was spread among them that a great paper
manufacturer, of the name of Reveillon, had proposed, on some occasion, that their wages should be
lowered to 15 sous a day. Inflamed at once into
rage, & without inquiring into it's truth, they flew
to his house in vast numbers, destroyed everything
in it, and in his magazines & work shops, without
secreting however a pin's worth to themselves, and
were continuing this work of devastation when the
regular troops were called in. Admonitions being
disregarded, they were of necessity fired on, and a
regular action ensued, in which about 100. of them

were killed, before the rest would disperse. There had rarely passed a year without such a riot in some part or other of the Kingdom; and this is distinguished only as cotemporary with the revolution, altho' not produced by it.

The States General were opened on the 5th. of May 89. by speeches from the King, the Garde des Sceaux Lamoignon, and Mr. Necker. The last was thought to trip too lightly over the constitutional reformations which were expected. His notices of them in this speech were not as full as in his previous 'Rapport au Roi.' This was observed to his disadvantage. But much allowance should have been made for the situation in which he was placed between his own counsels, and those of the ministers and party of the court. Overruled in his own opinions, compelled to deliver, and to gloss over those of his opponents, and even to keep their secrets, he could not come forward in his own attitude.

The composition of the assembly, altho' equivalent on the whole to what had been expected, was something different in it's elements. It had been supposed that a superior education would carry into the scale of the Commons a respectable portion of the Noblesse. It did so as to those of Paris, of it's vicinity and of the other considerable cities, whose greater intercourse with enlightened society had liberalized their minds, and prepared them to advance up to the measure of the times. But the Noblesse of the country, which constituted two thirds of that body, were far in their rear. Residing constantly on their patrimonial feuds, and familiarized by daily habit with Seigneurial powers and practices, they had not yet learned to suspect their inconsistence with reason and right. They were willing to submit to equality of taxation, but not to descend from their rank and prerogatives to be incorporated in session with the tiers etat. Among the clergy, on the other hand, it had been apprehended that the higher orders of the hierarchy, by their wealth and connections, would have carried the elections generally. But it proved that in most cases the lower clergy had obtained the popular majorities. These consisted of the Curés, sons of the peasantry who had been employed to do all the drudgery of parochial services for 10. 20. or 30 Louis a year; while their superiors were consuming their princely revenues in palaces of luxury & indolence.

The objects for which this body was convened being of the first order of importance, I felt it very interesting to understand the views of the parties of which it was composed, and especially the ideas prevalent as to the organization contemplated for their government. I went therefore daily from Paris to Versailles, and attended their debates, generally till the hour of adjournment. Those of the Noblesse were impassioned and tempestuous. They had some able men on both sides, and actuated by equal zeal. The debates of the Commons were temperate, rational and inflexibly firm. As preliminary to all other business, the awful questions came on, Shall the States sit in one, or in distinct apartments? And shall they vote by heads or houses? The opposition was soon found to consist of the Episcopal

order among the clergy, and two thirds of the Noblesse; while the tiers etat were, to a man, united
and determined.   After various propositions of compromise had failed, the Commons undertook to cut
the Gordian knot.   The Abbe Sieyes, the most
logical head of the nation (author of the pamphlet
Qu'est ce que le tiers etat? which had electrified that
country, as Paine's *Common sense* did us) after an
impressive speech on the 10th of June, moved that
a last invitation should be sent to the Nobles and
Clergy, to attend in the Hall of the States, collect-
ively or individually for the verification of powers,
to which the commons would proceed immediately,
either in their presence or absence.   This verification being finished, a motion was made, on the 15th.
that they should constitute themselves a National
assembly; which was decided on the 17th. by a
majority of four fifths.   During the debates on this
question, about twenty of the Curés had joined them,
and a proposition was made in the chamber of the
clergy that their whole body should join them.
This was rejected at first by a small majority only;
but, being afterwards somewhat modified, it was
decided affirmatively, by a majority of eleven.
While this was under debate and unknown to the
court, to wit, on the 19th. a council was held in the
afternoon at Marly, wherein it was proposed that
the King should interpose by a declaration of his
sentiments, in a *seance royale*.   A form of declaration
was proposed by Necker, which, while it censured in
general the proceedings both of the Nobles and Commons, announced the King's views, such as substan-

tially to coincide with the Commons.   It was agreed
to in council, the *seance* was fixed for the 22d. the
meetings of the States were till then to be suspended,
and everything, in the meantime, kept secret.   The
members the next morning (20th.) repairing to their
house as usual, found the doors shut and guarded, a
proclamation posted up for a seance royale on the
22d. and a suspension of their meetings in the meantime.   Concluding that their dissolution was now to
take place, they repaired to a building called the
" Jeu de paume " (or Tennis court) and there bound
themselves by oath to each other, never to separate
of their own accord, till they had settled a constitution for the nation, on a solid basis, and if separated
by force, that they would reassemble in some other
place.   The next day they met in the church of St.
Louis, and were joined by a majority of the clergy.
The heads of the Aristocracy saw that all was lost
without some bold exertion.   The King was still at
Marly.   Nobody was permitted to approach him
but their friends.   He was assailed by falsehoods in
all shapes.   He was made to believe that the Commons were about to absolve the army from their
oath of fidelity to him, and to raise their pay.   The
court party were now all rage and desperate.   They
procured a committee to be held consisting of the
King and his ministers, to which Monsieur & the
Count d' Artois should be admitted.   At this committee the latter attacked Mr. Necker personally,
arraigned his declaration, and proposed one which
some of his prompters had put into his hands.   Mr.
Necker was brow-beaten and intimidated, and the

King shaken. He determined that the two plans
should be deliberated on the next day and the
seance royale put off a day longer. This encouraged
a fiercer attack on Mr. Necker the next day. His
draught of a declaration was entirely broken up, &
that of the Count d'Artois inserted into it. Himself
and Montmorin offered their resignation, which was
refused, the Count d'Artois saying to Mr. Necker
"No sir, you must be kept as the hostage; we hold
you responsible for all the ill which shall happen."
This change of plan was immediately whispered
without doors. The Noblesse were in triumph; the
people in consternation. I was quite alarmed at
this state of things. The soldiery had not yet indicated which side they should take, and that which
they should support would be sure to prevail. I
considered a successful reformation of government
in France, as ensuring a general reformation thro
Europe, and the resurrection, to a new life, of their
people, now ground to dust by the abuses of the
governing powers. I was much acquainted with
the leading patriots of the assembly. Being from a
country which had successfully passed thro' a similar
reformation, they were disposed to my acquaintance,
and had some confidence in me. I urged most
strenuously an immediate compromise; to secure
what the government was now ready to yield, and
trust to future occasions for what might still be
wanting. It was well understood that the King
would grant at this time 1. Freedom of the person
by Habeas corpus. 2. Freedom of conscience. 3.
Freedom of the press. 4. Trial by jury. 5. A repre-

sentative legislature. 6. Annual meetings. 7. The
origination of laws. 8. The exclusive right of taxation and appropriation. And 9. The responsibility
of ministers; and with the exercise of these powers
they would obtain in future whatever might be further necessary to improve and preserve their constitution. They thought otherwise however, and
events have proved their lamentable error. For
after 30. years of war, foreign and domestic, the loss
of millions of lives, the prostration of private happiness, and foreign subjugation of their own country
for a time, they have obtained no more, nor even
that securely. They were unconscious of (for who
could foresee?) the melancholy sequel of their well-
meant perseverance; that their physical force would
be usurped by a first tyrant to trample on the independance, and even the existence, of other nations:
that this would afford fatal example for the atrocious
conspiracy of Kings against their people; would
generate their unholy and homicide alliance to make
common cause among themselves, and to crush, by
the power of the whole, the efforts of any part, to
moderate their abuses and oppressions.

When the King passed, the next day, thro' the
lane formed from the Chateau to the Hotel des etats,
there was a dead silence. He was about an hour in
the House delivering his speech & declaration. On
his coming out a feeble cry of "Vive le Roy" was
raised by some children, but the people remained
silent & sullen. In the close of his speech he
had ordered that the members should follow him,
& resume their deliberations the next day. The

Noblesse followed him, and so did the clergy, except about thirty, who, with the tiers, remained in the room, and entered into deliberation. They protested against what the King had done, adhered to all their former proceedings, and resolved the inviolability of their own persons. An officer came to order them out of the room in the King's name. "Tell those who sent you, said Mirabeau, that we shall not move hence but at our own will, or the point of the bayonet." In the afternoon the people, uneasy, began to assemble in great numbers in the courts, and vicinities of the palace. This produced alarm. The Queen sent for Mr. Necker. He was conducted amidst the shouts and acclamations of the multitude. who filled all the apartments of the palace. He was a few minutes only with the queen, and what passed between them did not transpire. The King went out to ride. He passed thro' the crowd to his carriage and into it, without being in the least noticed. As Mr. Neckar followed him universal acclamations were raised of "vive Monsr. Neckar, vive le sauveur de la France opprimée." He was conducted back to his house with the same demonstrations of affection and anxiety. About 200. deputies of the Tiers, catching the enthusiasm of the moment, went to his house, and extorted from him a promise that he would not resign. On the 25th. 48. of the Nobles joined the tiers, & among them the D. of Orleans. There were then with them 164 members of the Clergy, altho' the minority of that body still sat apart & called themselves the chamber of the clergy. On the 26th. the Archbp. of Paris joined the tiers, as did some others of the clergy and of the Noblesse.

These proceedings had thrown the people into violent ferment. It gained the souldiery, first of the French guards, extended to those of every other denomination, except the Swiss, and even to the body guards of the King. They began to quit their barracks, to assemble in squads, to declare they would defend the life of the King, but would not be the murderers of their fellow-citizens. They called themselves the souldiers *of the nation*, and left now no doubt on which side they would be, in case of rupture. Similar accounts came in from the troops in other parts of the kingdom, giving good reason to believe they would side with their fathers and brothers rather than with their officers. The operation of this medicine at Versailles was as sudden as it was powerful. The alarm there was so compleat that in the afternoon of the 27th. the King wrote with his own hand letters to the Presidents of the clergy and Nobles, engaging them immediately to join the Tiers. These two bodies were debating & hesitating when notes from the Ct. d' Artois decided their compliance. They went in a body and took their seats with the tiers, and thus rendered the union of the orders in one chamber compleat.

The Assembly now entered on the business of their mission, and first proceeded to arrange the order in which they would take up the heads of their constitution, as follows:

First, and as Preliminary to the whole a general Declaration of the Rights of Man. Then specifically the Principles of the Monarchy; rights of the Nation; rights of the King; rights of the citizens; organization & rights of the National assembly; forms necessary for the enactment of laws; organization & functions of the provincial & municipal assemblies; duties and limits of the Judiciary power; functions & duties of the military power.

A declaration of the rights of man, as the preliminary of their work, was accordingly prepared and proposed by the Marquis de la Fayette.

But the quiet of their march was soon disturbed by information that troops, and particularly the foreign troops, were advancing on Paris from various quarters. The King had been probably advised to this on the pretext of preserving peace in Paris. But his advisers were believed to have other things in contemplation. The Marshal de Broglio was appointed to their command, a high flying aristocrat, cool and capable of everything. Some of the French guards were soon arrested, under other pretexts, but really on account of their dispositions in favor of the National cause. The people of Paris forced their prison, liberated them, and sent a deputation to the Assembly to solicit a pardon. The Assembly recommended peace and order to the people of Paris, the prisoners to the King, and asked from him the removal of the troops. His answer was negative and dry, saying they might remove themselves, if they pleased, to Noyons or Soissons. In the meantime these troops, to the number of twenty or thirty thousand, had arrived and were posted in, and between Paris and Versailles. The bridges and passes were guarded. At three o'clock in the afternoon of the 11th July the Count de la Luzerne was sent to notify Mr. Neckar of his dismission, and to enjoin him to retire instantly without saying a word of it to anybody. He went home, dined, and proposed to his wife a visit to a friend, but went in fact to his country house at St. Ouen, and at midnight set out for Brussels. This was not known till the next day, 12th when the whole ministry was changed, except Ville-deuil, of the Domestic department, and Barenton, Garde des sceaux. The changes were as follows:

The Baron de Breteuil, president of the council of finance; de la Galaisiere, Comptroller general in the room of Mr. Neckar; the Marshal de Broglio, minister of War, & Foulon under him in the room of Puy-Segur; the Duke de la Vauguyon, minister of foreign affairs instead of the Ct. de Montmorin; de La Porte, minister of Marine, in place of the Ct. de la Luzerne; St. Priest was also removed from the council. Luzerne and Puy-Segur had been strongly of the Aristocratic party in the Council, but they were not considered as equal to the work now to be done. The King was now compleatly in the hands of men, the principal among whom had been noted thro' their lives for the Turkish despotism of their characters, and who were associated around the King as proper instruments for what was to be executed. The news of this change began to be known at Paris about 1. or 2. o'clock. In the afternoon a body of about 100 German cavalry were advanced and drawn up in the Place Louis XV. and about 200. Swiss posted at a little distance in their rear. This drew people to the

spot, who thus accidentally found themselves in
front of the troops, merely at first as spectators;
but as their numbers increased, their indignation
rose. They retired a few steps, and posted themselves on and behind large piles of stones, large and
small, collected in that Place for a bridge which was
to be built adjacent to it. In this position, happen-
ing to be in my carriage on a visit, I passed thro' the
lane they had formed, without interruption. But
the moment after I had passed, the people attacked
the cavalry with stones. They charged, but the ad-
vantageous position of the people, and the showers
of stones obliged the horse to retire, and quit the
field altogether, leaving one of their number on the
ground, & the Swiss in their rear not moving to their
aid. This was the signal for universal insurrection,
and this body of cavalry, to avoid being massacred,
retired towards Versailles. The people now armed
themselves with such weapons as they could find in
armorer's shops and private houses, and with blud-
geons, and were roaming all night thro' all parts of
the city, without any decided object. The next day
(13th.) the assembly pressed on the king to send
away the troops, to permit the Bourgeosie of Paris
to arm for the preservation of order in the city, and
offer[ed] to send a deputation from their body to
tranquillize them; but their propositions were refused. A committee of magistrates and electors of
the city are appointed by those bodies to take upon
them it's government. The people, now openly
joined by the French guards, force the prison of St.
Lazare, release all the prisoners, and take a great

store of corn, which they carry to the Corn-market.
Here they get some arms, and the French guards
begin to form & train them. The City-committee
determined to raise 48.000 Bourgeoise, or rather to
restrain their numbers to 48.000. On the 14th.
they send one of their members (Mons. de Corny) to
the Hotel des Invalides, to ask arms for their Garde-
Bourgeoise. He was followed by, and he found
there a great collection of people. The Governor of
the Invalids came out and represented the impossibility of his delivering arms without the orders of
those from whom he received them. De Corny advised the people then to retire, and retired himself;
but the people took possession of the arms. It was
remarkable that not only the Invalids themselves
made no opposition, but that a body of 5000. foreign troops, within 400. yards, never stirred. M. de
Corny and five others were then sent to ask arms of
M. de Launay, governor of the Bastile. They found
a great collection of people already before the place,
and they immediately planted a flag of truce, which
was answered by a like flag hoisted on the Parapet.
The deputation prevailed on the people to fall back
a little, advanced themselves to make their demand
of the Governor, and in that instant a discharge from
the Bastile killed four persons, of those nearest to
the deputies. The deputies retired. I happened to
be at the house of M. de Corny when he returned
to it, and received from him a narrative of these
transactions. On the retirement of the deputies,
the people rushed forward & almost in an instant
were in possession of a fortification defended by 100.

men of infinite strength, which in other times had
stood several regular sieges, and had never been
taken. How they forced their entrance has never
been explained. They took all the arms, discharged
the prisoners, and such of the garrison as were not
killed in the first moment of fury, carried the Governor and Lt. Governor to the Place de Grève (the
place of public execution) cut off their heads, and
sent them thro' the city in triumph to the Palais
royal. About the same instant a treacherous correspondence having been discovered in M. de Flesselles,
prevot des marchands, they seized him in the Hotel
de Ville where he was in the execution of his office,
and cut off his head. These events carried imper-
fectly to Versailles were the subject of two successive
deputations from the assembly to the king, to both of
which he gave dry and hard answers for nobody had
as yet been permitted to inform him truly and fully
of what had passed at Paris. But at night the Duke
de Liancourt forced his way into the king's bed
chamber, and obliged him to hear a full and ani-
mated detail of the disasters of the day in Paris.
He went to bed fearfully impressed. The decapita-
tion of de Launai worked powerfully thro' the night
on the whole aristocratic party, insomuch that, in
the morning, those of the greatest influence on the
Count d'Artois represented to him the absolute necessity that the king should give up everything to the
Assembly. This according with the dispositions of
the king, he went about 11. o'clock, accompanied
only by his brothers, to the Assembly, & there read
to them a speech, in which he asked their interposi-

tion to re-establish order.   Altho' couched in terms
of some caution, yet the manner in which it was delivered made it evident that it was meant as a surrender at discretion.   He returned to the Chateau
afoot, accompanied by the assembly.   They sent off
a deputation to quiet Paris, at the head of which was
the Marquis de la Fayette who had, the same morning, been named Commandant en chef of the Milice
Bourgeoise, and Mons Bailly, former President of
the States General, was called for as Prevot des marchands.   The demolition of the Bastile was now
ordered and begun.   A body of the Swiss guards of
the regiment of Ventimille, and the city horse guards
joined the people.   The alarm at Versailles increased.
The foreign troops were ordered off instantly.   Every
minister resigned.   The king confirmed Bailly as
Prevot des Marchands, wrote to Mr. Neckar to recall
him, sent his letter open to the assembly, to be forwarded by them, and invited them to go with him to
Paris the next day, to satisfy the city of his dispositions; and that night, and the next morning the
Count d'Artois and M. de Montesson a deputy connected with him, Madame de Polignac, Madame de
Guiche, and the Count de Vaudreuil, favorites of
the queen, the Abbe de Vermont, her confessor, the
Prince of Condé and Duke of Bourbon fled.   The
king came to Paris, leaving the queen in consternation for his return.   Omitting the less important
figures of the procession, the king's carriage was in
the center, on each side of it the assembly, in two
ranks afoot, at their head the M. de la Fayette, as
Commander-in-chief, on horseback, and Bourgeois

guards before and behind.   About 60.000 citizens of
all forms and conditions, armed with the muskets of
the Bastile and Invalids, as far as they would go,
the rest with pistols, swords, pikes, pruning hooks,
scythes, &c. lined all the streets thro' which the
procession passed, and with the crowds of people in
the streets, doors & windows, saluted them everywhere with cries of "vive la nation," but not a
single "vive le roy" was heard.   The King landed
at the Hotel de Ville.   There M. Bailly presented
and put into his hat the popular cockade, and addressed him.   The King being unprepared, and unable to answer, Bailly went to him, gathered from
him some scraps of sentences, and made out an answer, which he delivered to the audience as from the
king.   On their return the popular cries were "vive
le roy et la nation."   He was conducted by a garde
bourgeoise to his palace at Versailles, & thus concluded an amende honorable as no sovereign ever
made, and no people ever received.

And here again was lost another precious occasion
of sparing to France the crimes and cruelties thro'
which she has since passed, and to Europe, & finally
America the evils which flowed on them also from
this mortal source.   The king was now become a
passive machine in the hands of the National Assembly, and had he been left to himself, he would have
willingly acquiesced in whatever they should devise
as best for the nation.   A wise constitution would
have been formed, hereditary in his line, himself
placed at it's head, with powers so large as to enable
him to do all the good of his station, and so limited

as to restrain him from it's abuse. This he would
have faithfully administered, and more than this I
do not believe he ever wished. But he had a Queen
of absolute sway over his weak mind, and timid virtue; and of a character the reverse of his in all points.
This angel, as gaudily painted in the rhapsodies of
the Rhetor Burke, with some smartness of fancy, but
no sound sense was proud, disdainful of restraint,
indignant at all obstacles to her will, eager in the
pursuit of pleasure, and firm enough to hold to her
desires, or perish in their wreck. Her inordinate
gambling and dissipations, with those of the Count
d'Artois and others of her clique, had been a sensible
item in the exhaustion of the treasury, which called
into action the reforming hand of the nation; and
her opposition to it her inflexible perverseness, and
dauntless spirit, led herself to the Guillotine, & drew
the king on with her, and plunged the world into
crimes & calamities which will forever stain the
pages of modern history. I have ever believed that
had there been no queen, there would have been no
revolution. No force would have been provoked
nor exercised. The king would have gone hand in
hand with the wisdom of his sounder counsellors,
who, guided by the increased lights of the age, wished
only, with the same pace, to advance the principles
of their social institution. The deed which closed
the mortal course of these sovereigns, I shall neither
approve nor condemn. I am not prepared to say
that the first magistrate of a nation cannot commit
treason against his country, or is unamenable to it's
punishment: nor yet that where there is no written

law, no regulated tribunal, there is not a law in our
hearts, and a power in our hands, given for righteous
employment in maintaining right, and redressing
wrong. Of those who judged the king, many thought
him wilfully criminal, many that his existence would
keep the nation in perpetual conflict with the horde
of kings, who would war against a regeneration
which might come home to themselves, and that it
were better that one should die than all. I should
not have voted with this portion of the legislature.
I should have shut up the Queen in a Convent, putting harm out of her power, and placed the king in
his station, investing him with limited powers, which
I verily believe he would have honestly exercised,
according to the measure of his understanding. In
this way no void would have been created, courting
the usurpation of a military adventurer, nor occasion given for those enormities which demoralized
the nations of the world, and destroyed, and is yet
to destroy millions and millions of it's inhabitants.
There are three epochs in history signalized by the
total extinction of national morality. The first was
of the successors of Alexander, not omitting himself.
The next the successors of the first Cæsar, the third
our own age. This was begun by the partition of
Poland followed by that of the treaty of Pilnitz
next the conflagration of Copenhagen; then the
enormities of Bonaparte partitioning the earth at his
will, and devastating it with fire and sword; now
the conspiracy of kings, the successors of Bonaparte,
blasphemously calling themselves the Holy Alliance,
and treading in the footsteps of their incarcerated

leader, not yet indeed usurping the government of other nations avowedly and in detail, but controuling by their armies the forms in which they will permit them to be governed; and reserving in petto the order and extent of the usurpations further medi- tated. But I will return from a digression, antici- pated too in time, into which I have been led by reflection on the criminal passions which refused to the world a favorable occasion of saving it from the afflictions it has since suffered.

M. Necker had reached Basle before he was over- taken by the letter of the king, inviting him back to resume the office he had recently left. He returned immediately, and all the other ministers having re- signed, a new administration was named, to wit St. Priest & Montmorin were restored; the Archbishop of Bordeaux was appointed Garde des sceaux; La Tour du Pin Minister of War; La Luzerne Minister of Marine. This last was believed to have been effected by the friendship of Montmorin; for altho' differing in politics, they continued firm in friend- ship, & Luzerne, altho' not an able man was thought an honest one. And the Prince of Bauvau was taken into the Council.

Seven princes of the blood royal, six ex-ministers, and many of the high Noblesse having fled, and the present ministers, except Luzerne, being all of the popular party, all the functionaries of government moved for the present in perfect harmony.

In the evening of Aug. 4. and on the motion of the Viscount de Noailles brother in law of La Fay- ette, the assembly abolished all titles of rank, all the

abusive privileges of feudalism, the tythes and casu-
als of the clergy, all provincial privileges, and, in fine,
the Feudal regimen generally.   To the suppression
of tythes the Abbe Sieyes was vehemently opposed;
but his learned and logical arguments were un-
heeded, and his estimation lessened by a contrast
of his egoism (for he was beneficed on them) with the
generous abandonment of rights by the other members of the assembly.   Many days were employed in
putting into the form of laws the numerous demoli-
tions of ancient abuses; which done, they proceeded
to the preliminary work of a Declaration of rights.
There being much concord of sentiment on the elements of this instrument, it was liberally framed,
and passed with a very general approbation.   They
then appointed a Committee for the reduction of a
projet of a Constitution, at the head of which was
the Archbishop of Bordeaux.   I received from him,
as Chairman of the Commitee a letter of July 20.
requesting me to attend and assist at their deliberations; but I excused myself on the obvious considerations that my mission was to the king as Chief
Magistrate of the nation, that my duties were limited
to the concerns of my own country, and forbade me
to intermeddle with the internal transactions of that
in which I had been received under a specific character only.   Their plan of a constitution was discussed
in sections, and so reported from time to time, as
agreed to by the Committee.   The first respected the
general frame of the government; and that this
should be formed into three departments, Executive,
Legislative and Judiciary was generally agreed.   But

when they proceeded to subordinate developments, many and various shades of opinion came into conflict, and schism, strongly marked, broke the Patriots into fragments of very discordant principles. The first question Whether there should be a king, met with no open opposition, and it was readily agreed that the government of France should be monarchical & hereditary. Shall the king have a negative on the laws? shall that negative be absolute, or suspensive only? Shall there be two chambers of legislation? or one only? If two, shall one of them be hereditary? or for life? or for a fixed term? and named by the king? or elected by the people? These questions found strong differences of opinion, and produced repulsive combinations among the Patriots. The Aristocracy was cemented by a common principle of preserving the ancient regime, or whatever should be nearest to it. Making this their Polar star, they moved in phalanx, gave preponderance on every question to the minorities of the Patriots, and always to those who advocated the least change. The features of the new constitution were thus assuming a fearful aspect, and great alarm was produced among the honest patriots by these dissensions in their ranks. In this uneasy state of things, I received one day a note from the Marquis de la Fayette, informing me that he should bring a party of six or eight friends to ask a dinner of me the next day. I assured him of their welcome. When they arrived, they were La Fayette himself, Duport, Barnave, Alexander La Meth, Blacon, Mounier, Maubourg, and Dagout. These were leading patriots,

of honest but differing opinions sensible of the necessity of effecting a coalition by mutual sacrifices,
knowing each other, and not afraid therefore to un-
bosom themselves mutually.   This last was a material principle in the selection.   With this view the
Marquis had invited the conference and had fixed the
time & place inadvertently as to the embarrassment
under which it might place me.   The cloth being removed and wine set on the table, after the American
manner, the Marquis introduced the objects of the
conference by summarily reminding them of the
state of things in the Assembly, the course which
the principles of the constitution were taking, and
the inevitable result, unless checked by more concord
among the Patriots themselves.   He observed that
altho' he also had his opinion, he was ready to sacrifice it to that of his brethren of the same cause: but
that a common opinion must now be formed, or the
Aristocracy would carry everything, and that whatever they should now agree on, he, at the head of the
National force, would maintain.   The discussions
began at the hour of four, and were continued till
ten o'clock in the evening; during which time I was
a silent witness to a coolness and candor of argument unusual in the conflicts of political opinion;
to a logical reasoning, and chaste eloquence, disfig-
ured by no gaudy tinsel of rhetoric or declamation,
and truly worthy of being placed in parallel with the
finest dialogues of antiquity, as handed to us by
Xenophon, by Plato and Cicero.   The result was an
agreement that the king should have a suspensive
veto on the laws, that the legislature should be com-

posed of a single body only, & that to be chosen by
the people.   This Concordate decided the fate of the
constitution.   The Patriots all rallied to the principles thus settled, carried every question agreeably
to them, and reduced the Aristocracy to insignificance and impotence.   But duties of exculpation
were now incumbent on me.   I waited on Count
Montmorin the next morning, and explained to him
with truth and candor how it had happened that my
house had been made the scene of conferences of such
a character.   He told me he already knew everything
which had passed, that, so far from taking umbrage
at the use made of my house on that occasion, he
earnestly wished I would habitually assist at such
conferences, being sure I should be useful in moderat-
ing the warmer spirits, and promoting a wholesome
and practicable reformation only.   I told him I
knew too well the duties I owed to the king, to the
nation, and to my own country to take any part in
councils concerning their internal government, and
that I should persevere with care in the character of
a neutral and passive spectator, with wishes only
and very sincere ones, that those measures might
prevail which would be for the greatest good of the
nation.   I have no doubt indeed that this conference
was previously known and approved by this honest
minister, who was in confidence and communication
with the patriots, and wished for a reasonable reform
of the Constitution.

Here I discontinue my relation of the French revolution.   The minuteness with which I have so far
given it's details is disproportioned to the general

scale of my narrative. But I have thought it justified by the interest which the whole world must take in this revolution. As yet we are but in the first chapter of it's history. The appeal to the rights of man, which had been made in the U S. was taken up by France, first of the European nations. From her the spirit has spread over those of the South. The tyrants of the North have allied indeed against it, but it is irresistible. Their opposition will only multiply it's millions of human victims; their own satellites will catch it, and the condition of man thro' the civilized world will be finally and greatly ameliorated. This is a wonderful instance of great events from small causes. So inscrutable is the arrangement of causes & consequences in this world that a two-penny duty on tea, unjustly imposed in a sequestered part of it, changes the condition of all it's inhabitants. I have been more minute in relating the early transactions of this regeneration because I was in circumstances peculiarly favorable for a knowledge of the truth. Possessing the confidence and intimacy of the leading patriots, & more than all of the Marquis Fayette, their head and Atlas, who had no secrets from me, I learnt with correctness the views & proceedings of that party; while my intercourse with the diplomatic missionaries of Europe at Paris, all of them with the court, and eager in prying into it's councils and proceedings, gave me a knolege of these also. My information was always and immediately committed to writing, in letters to Mr. Jay, and often to my friends, and a recurrence to these letters now insures me against errors of memory.

These opportunities of information ceased at this period, with my retirement from this interesting scene of action. I had been more than a year soliciting leave to go home with a view to place my daughters in the society & care of their friends, and to return for a short time to my station at Paris. But the metamorphosis thro' which our government was then passing from it's Chrysalid to it's Organic form suspended it's action in a great degree; and it was not till the last of August that I received the permission I had asked.—And here I cannot leave this great and good country without expressing my sense of it's preeminence of character among the nations of the earth. A more benevolent people, I have never known, nor greater warmth & devotedness in their select friendships. Their kindness and accommodation to strangers is unparalleled, and the hospitality of Paris is beyond anything I had conceived to be practicable in a large city. Their eminence too in science, the communicative dispositions of their scientific men, the politeness of the general manners, the ease and vivacity of their conversation, give a charm to their society to be found nowhere else. In a comparison of this with other countries we have the proof of primacy, which was given to Themistocles after the battle of Salamis. Every general voted to himself the first reward of valor, and the second to Themistocles. So ask the travelled inhabitant of any nation, In what country on earth would you rather live?—Certainly in my own, where are all my friends, my relations, and the earliest & sweetest affections and recollections of my life. Which would be your second choice? France.

On the 26th. of Sep. I left Paris for Havre, where I was detained by contrary winds until the 8th. of Oct. On that day, and the 9th. I crossed over to Cowes, where I had engaged the *Clermont*, Capt. Colley, to touch for me. She did so, but here again we were detained by contrary winds until the 22d. when we embarked and landed at Norfolk on the 23d. of November. On my way home I passed some days at Eppington in Chesterfield, the residence of my friend and connection, Mr. Eppes, and, while there, I received a letter from the President, Genl. Washington, by express, covering an appointment to be Secretary of State. I received it with real regret. My wish had been to return to Paris, where I had left my household establishment, as if there myself, and to see the end of the Revolution, which, I then thought would be certainly and happily closed in less than a year. I then meant to return home, to withdraw from Political life, into which I had been impresed by the circumstances of the times, to sink into the bosom of my family and friends, and devote myself to studies more congenial to my mind. In my answer of Dec. 15. I expressed these dispositions candidly to the President, and my preference of a return to Paris; but assured him that if it was believed I could be more useful in the administration of the government, I would sacrifice my own inclinations without hesitation, and repair to that destination; this I left to his decision. I arrived at Monticello on the 23d. of Dec. where I received a second letter from the President, expressing his continued wish that I should take my station there, but leaving me still at liberty to con-

tinue in my former office, if I could not reconcile myself to that now proposed. This silenced my reluctance, and I accepted the new appointment.

In the interval of my stay at home my eldest
daughter had been happily married to the eldest son [1]
of the Tuckahoe branch of Randolphs, a young gentleman of genius, science and honorable mind, who
afterwards filled a dignified station in the General
Government, & the most dignified in his own State.
I left Monticello on the 1st of March 1790. for New
York. At Philadelphia I called on the venerable and
beloved Franklin. He was then on the bed of sickness from which he never rose. My recent return
from a country in which he had left so many friends,
and the perilous convulsions to which they had been
exposed, revived all his anxieties to know what part
they had taken, what had been their course, and what
their fate. He went over all in succession, with a
rapidity and animation almost too much for his
strength. When all his inquiries were satisfied, and
a pause took place, I told him I had learnt with much
pleasure that, since his return to America, he had
been occupied in preparing for the world the history
of his own life. I cannot say much of that, said he;
but I will give you a sample of what I shall leave:
and he directed his little grandson (William Bache)
who was standing by the bedside, to hand him a paper
from the table to which he pointed. He did so; and
the Doctr. putting it into my hands, desired me to
take it and read it at my leisure. It was about a
quire of folio paper, written in a large and running

[1] Thomas Mann Randolph.

hand very like his own. I looked into it slightly, then shut it and said I would accept his permission to read it and would carefully return it. He said, "no, keep it." Not certain of his meaning, I again looked into it, folded it for my pocket, and said again, I would certainly return it. "No," said he, "keep it." I put it into my pocket, and shortly after took leave of him. He died on the 17th, of the ensuing month of April; and as I understood that he had bequeathed all his papers to his grandson William Temple Franklin, I immediately wrote to Mr. Franklin to inform him I possessed this paper, which I should consider as his property, and would deliver to his order. He came on immediately to New York, called on me for it, and I delivered it to him. As he put it into his pocket, he said carelessly he had either the original, or another copy of it, I do not recollect which. This last expression struck my attention forcibly, and for the first time suggested to me the thought that Dr. Franklin had meant it as a confidential deposit in my hands, and that I had done wrong in parting from it. I have not yet seen the collection he published of Dr. Franklin's works,[1] and therefore know not if this is among them. I have been told it is not. It contained a narrative of the negotiations between Dr. Franklin and the British Ministry, when he was endeavoring to prevent the contest of arms which followed. The negotiation was brought about by the intervention of Ld. Howe and his sister, who, I believe, was called Lady Howe, but I may misremember her title. Ld. Howe seems

---

[1] It was printed in that edition.

to have been friendly to America, and exceedingly
anxious to prevent a rupture. His intimacy with Dr.
Franklin, and his position with the Ministry induced
him to undertake a mediation between them; in
which his sister seemed to have been associated.
They carried from one to the other, backwards and
forwards, the several propositions and answers which
past, and seconded with their own intercessions the
importance of mutual sacrifices to preserve the peace
& connection of the two countries. I remember that
Ld. North's answers were dry, unyielding, in the
spirit of unconditional submission, and betrayed an
absolute indifference to the occurrence of a rupture;
and he said to the mediators distinctly, at last that
"a rebellion was not to be deprecated on the part of
Great Britain; that the confiscations it would produce would provide for many of their friends." [1]
This expression was reported by the mediators to
Dr. Franklin, and indicated so cool and calculated a
purpose in the Ministry, as to render compromise
hopeless, and the negotiation was discontinued. If
this is not among the papers published, we ask what
has become of it? I delivered it with my own hands
into those of Temple Franklin. It certainly established views so atrocious in the British government
that it's suppression would to them be worth a great
price. But could the grandson of Dr. Franklin be in
such degree an accomplice in the parricide of the
memory of his immortal grandfather? The suspension for more than 20. years of the general publication

[1] Neither this expression, nor any of Lord North's, were given in
Franklin's narrative. *Cf.* Bigelow's *Writings of Franklin*, v. 440.

bequeathed and confided to him, produced for awhile hard suspicions against him: and if at last all are not published, a part of these suspicions may remain with some.

I arrived at New York on the 21st. of Mar. where Congress was in session.

So far July 29. 21.